SPIRITUAL SIM

SPIRITUAL SIMPLICITY

Doing Less, Loving More

CHIP INGRAM

WITH CHRIS TIEGREEN

HOWARD BOOKS

A DIVISION OF SIMON & SCHUSTER, INC.

New York   Nashville   London   Toronto   Sydney   New Delhi

Howard Books
A Division of Simon & Schuster, Inc.
1230 Avenue of the Americas
New York, NY 10020

First Howard Books hardcover edition January 2013

Scripture Quotations marked NIV are taken from THE HOLY BIBLE,
NEW INTERNATIONAL VERSION ®, NIV ® Copyright © 1973, 1978,
1984 by Biblica, Inc.™ Used by permission. All rights reserved worldwide.

Scripture quotations marked NASB are taken from the New American
Standard Bible. Copyright © 1960, 1962, 1963, 1968, 1971, 1972, 1973,
1975, 1977, 1995 by The Lockman Foundation, La Habra, Calif. All rights
reserved. http://www.lockman.org

HOWARD and colophon are trademarks of Simon & Schuster, Inc.

For information about special discounts for bulk purchases,
please contact Simon & Schuster Special Sales at 1-866-506-1949
or business@simonandschuster.com.

The Simon & Schuster Speakers Bureau can bring authors to your
live event. For more information or to book an event,
contact the Simon & Schuster Speakers Bureau at 1-866-248-3049
or visit our website at www.simonspeakers.com.

Designed by Davina Mock-Maniscalco

Manufactured in the United States of America

10   9   8   7   6   5   4   3   2   1

Library of Congress Cataloging-in-Publication Data

Ingram, Chip, 1954–
  Spiritual simplicity : doing less, loving more / by Chip Ingram.
    p. cm.
1. Simplicity—Religious aspects—Christianity. 2. Love—Religious aspects—
Christianity. 3. Bible. N.T. Corinthians, 1st—Criticism, interpretation, etc.
I. Title.
  BV4647.S48154 2013
  248.4—dc23

                                                               2012020617

ISBN 978-1-4391-3827-4
ISBN 978-1-4516-8852-8 (ebook)

I dedicate this to my teammates at Venture
Christian and Living on the Edge;
they have loved me and empowered God's purposes
in and through my life in a way I do not deserve,
but deeply appreciate.

Contents

Introduction

This book is for people who are tired, overextended, emotionally exhausted, and spiritually drained from doing too many good things. That's right—good things! In your effort to grow spiritually, help your children develop their gifts, hold down a job, serve at church, be a caring neighbor, stay in shape, coach Little League, and drive the car pool, you are personally maxed out. Weekends are packed with marathon sporting events and spiritual responsibilities. Weekdays start early, end late, and all too often find you eating fast food on the run.

But overextended, fast-paced, emotionally exhausting lifestyles are not reserved for the married with children. Singles find work to be a merciless taskmaster, and weekends are crammed with social and spiritual agendas that require half of Monday to recover.

I'm not immune to the madness. I live in one of the fastest-paced environments on the planet—Silicon Valley. As a pastor to people who leave their homes while it's still dark to launch the next product at Apple, Intel, Yahoo, Google, or HP, I see up close what happens to people's lives and relationships when life is fast, demands are high, and complexity is through the roof.

If you're looking for a quick fix on time management, seven easy steps to simplicity, or how to create margin in your life, this book isn't it. Most of us have tried all that, and it lasts a few days or a few weeks, at best. No, this book is for people who understand what they need to do, want desperately to do it, but find it next to impossible to break free of the complexity of *too many good and important things.*

This book isn't just theory. I don't sit in a plush office and pontificate about others being too busy. This was written over a two-and-a-half-year span after I came to the Silicon Valley to relaunch two churches that had merged. I was instantly greeted with major financial, facility, and staff issues, while at the same time my discipling ministry, Living on the Edge, was experiencing its most explosive growth since its inception. Then we discovered that Theresa, my wife, had cancer. I share this not to elicit your sympathy but simply to let you know that God allowed me to apply what is taught in this book at a spiritual "graduate course" level before I passed it on to you.

The thesis of this book is very simple:

Spiritual simplicity will never be achieved by strategic, managerial attempts to control our lives and schedules.

Spiritual simplicity will be achieved by *doing less* because we *love more.*

If that doesn't make complete sense right now, don't worry—it will. As you learn the practice of loving people in your relational network, you will experience a shift from complex to simple, from hurried to peaceful, from "never enough time" to "time enough for those you love."

> *Spiritual simplicity* will never be achieved by strategic, managerial attempts to control our lives and schedules.

I'm excited to begin this journey with you. I've added some questions at the end of the chapters to help you process, ponder, discuss with a friend or mate, and, most importantly, apply to your life. Old habits die hard; and deep, significant thinking always precedes long-term, lasting change. But if you are willing to apply some simple truths from God's Word, lasting change is within your reach.

ONE

All You Need Is Love

When I launched this series at our church, I knew I would be hitting some sensitive, raw nerves. The guilt and shame associated with pushing hard, passing your spouse like a ship in the night, and not giving your family the attention you know they need is a tough thing to face. I knew that "lecturing" these highly educated, professional people would not produce positive results. They may have the same basic needs as the rest of us, but the perceived pressure and demands of the high-tech world is like watching busyness on steroids.

So as people filed into the worship center, the worship team played the classic Beatles song "All You Need Is Love." No words, no singing, just an instrumental version that had everyone's toes tapping and boomers mouthing the words. The service would start in a few minutes, but I wanted to plant the idea in people's minds even before we started that "all you need is love."

You see, much of being driven, overextended, and always on an insane schedule is rooted in just the opposite of that song title. In fact, there's a dance that goes by many names all over the world that explains our spiritual and physical exhaustion and emotional fatigue. I call it the Silicon Valley Shuffle because that's where I live, but this dance is done in various forms from Omaha to Hong Kong. Regardless of the name you choose, there are four

> There are four steps to this dance that accelerate in rhythm and beat with every measure: *bigger, better, faster, more.*

steps to this dance that accelerate in rhythm and beat with every measure. See if you can recognize these steps: *bigger, better, faster, more.*

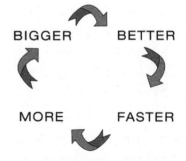

Four Words that Define Our Mind-Set

These four words drive our lives, our schedules, our relationships, and even our souls. They define the American mind-set. Our competitive businesses want to do things bigger, better, faster, and in greater quantity than their rivals. Our competitive job market prompts us to put in a few more hours and then a few more on top of that, because if we don't . . . well, anyone can be replaced. And our consumer wants and needs drive us in the same direction. We're never quite content with the status quo, so we're constantly looking to acquire whatever is bigger, better, faster, and more. That's how marketers appeal to us as consumers, and that's how we survive in this competitive culture as innovators, entrepreneurs, and difference makers. We're cutting-edge people in a world of opportunity.

Unfortunately, this mind-set spills over into our families too. If our kids are going to be really good at whatever we think they should be good at, then we've got to start them early. So we have three-year-olds playing in soccer leagues and sixth graders working with tutors to prepare for the SATs so they can get into the right college. The opportunities in our society are great, but the pressure and demand to take advantage of these opportunities—as many as possible—are overwhelming. We're constantly feeling pushed to be everything, do everything, and have everything; and as a result we live in a continual state of fatigue.

Are We Dancing Ourselves to Death?

Our attempts to "be it all," "do it all," and "have it all" have created a complex world that:

1. moves too fast

2. delivers too little

3. demands too much

We don't actually say we have to be it all, do it all, and have it all, of course. We may not even be conscious that we're chasing after these things. But our actions certainly reflect that pulsating drive. And when we do this dance—intentionally or not—we create a very complex world for ourselves. It's a world that moves too fast, delivers too little, and demands too much. Think about that:

> We create a world that moves too fast, delivers too little, and demands too much.

It moves too fast. Haven't you ever wished the clock would just stop so you could catch up on your work—or maybe just catch your breath? Do your days and weeks fly by and leave you in the dust? Have you ever wanted to jump off the merry-go-round of demands and activities but can't because it won't stop spinning? Those are very real symptoms that your world is moving too fast.

It delivers too little. Have you ever felt like you're pouring out more than you're taking in? That you're spinning your wheels? That the results of all your efforts are high activity but low relational connectivity? In quiet moments, does life feel disappointing and leaving you pretty unsatisfied? Those are symptoms that your world isn't delivering on its promises.

It demands too much. How many of us have crossed off everything on our to-do list? Isn't there unfinished business at the end of most days? Does your life seem like a cruel marathon—you see the finish line and keep running for it, but someone keeps moving it? Do you have trouble sleeping? Are you often anxious? Do you feel overwhelmed? These are symptoms of living in a world that demands too much—and that will suck the life out of you if you let it.

As I pastor in the Bay Area of California and minister across the United States, I see the impact of our highly driven, fast-paced, complex lifestyle. We end up with much fatigue, little margin, shallow relationships, fractured families, drifting marriages, painful loneliness, coping addictions, neglected kids, and generally hurting people.

If you think I'm exaggerating, let me share a not-so-atypical story of a young girl in a highly driven family. Her parents were convinced that education was the key to her success in life. So for four to five hours after school each day, she was required to do extra homework. Beginning in sixth grade, they hired a tutor to spend six hours with her every Saturday to prepare for her SAT and ACT exams. Their motives were to help their daughter, yet the competitive dance of bigger, better, faster, and more resulted in educational success and relational tragedy. She made perfect scores on both the SAT and the ACT and was awarded a full scholarship at an Ivy League school. Sounds like a great story, right? Wrong. Upon graduation, she changed her address and phone number three times to eliminate any contact with her parents. "Success" did a lot of relational damage. All of their "doing" didn't translate into "loving"—at least not in her eyes. In small and big ways, our drive for bigger-better-faster-more has taken over our lives.

As a result, our souls have a dis-ease. I don't mean a *disease*, as in a physical illness. I mean a *dis-ease*—a lack of ease. A nagging discomfort. A constant, underlying stress. This race we're running in order to get bigger, better, faster, and more is completely destroying our peace. We're losing our grounding. We don't know where we are or where we're going, or even how to go at a reasonable pace. Pretty soon, we realize that our relationships are coming unglued. We work mountains of hours, often for the sake of people we love, but end up with superficial relationships with those very same people because we've spent so much time working that we haven't invested in *them*. We've exchanged real, down-to-earth, quality relationships for money-bought privileges and perks. We've squeezed out the necessary time for friendships, marriage, children—even God. There's little authenticity or depth left—just enough to maintain our relationships superficially.

"I'll do that as soon as . . ." is the classic line of the over-committed person. We'll catch up on those relationships when this business deal is done or when we finish this project or when the kids get out of diapers and don't demand so much attention or when . . . But "when" never happens. Pretty soon, the kids are teenagers or leaving for college, you've forgotten how to have an in-depth conversation with your spouse, and your friends have all found other people to share their interests. Our "someday" thinking never really works out. Someday doesn't come unless we stop and decide to simplify our lives.

Glimmers of Hope

Once in a while, when people take a break, step back, and get alone with God, they get a glimpse of what's really happening. I've had multiple men and women tell me, "I've got to slow down. I've got to get some margin in my life. I can see the things that really matter slipping away." But it often takes a crisis to really do anything about it—a biopsy report or a car crash or a layoff—or sometimes God breaks in and encounters us on a rare vacation or a retreat. We suddenly see the speed of what's happening, and it seems ludicrous that we wouldn't have time for the God who made us, or for the person we vowed to grow with "until death do us part," or the people who share our DNA and need our love. But the Silicon Valley Shuffle, by whatever name, is lethal; we get caught up so completely in the demands that we often miss what matters most.

Is It Possible to Break Free?

Is it possible to break free from this trap—from the high-speed, high-pressure, high-demand, guilt-producing dis-ease of our complex lives? That's the question of this book—and the question we all need to ask ourselves if we're tired of being overextended and unfulfilled. I believe the answer is yes, it *is* possible to run the race at an entirely different, more meaningful speed. Not only is it possible, it's absolutely necessary.

Why We Do the Things We Do

Imagine this: You've been having an unexplained fever, along with some serious aches and pains. And even though you hate going to the doctor, you're worried enough to schedule an appointment. Something might really be wrong. So you get to the doctor's office, worried about all the possibilities. The doctor walks in and says hello, doesn't even wait for you to finish explaining your symptoms, and immediately grabs some pills off the shelf and says, "Here, take some of these and see if they work."

You say, "Wait a minute, doc! Are you sure that's the right way to deal with my problem?"

"Hmm, maybe not," he answers. "Just to be on the safe side, let's go ahead and schedule surgery for six A.M. tomorrow."

Suddenly you don't have very much confidence in your doctor, do you? Where your physical health is concerned, one thing you want with your medical care is the right diagnosis. That's the key to treatment; you can't deal with the disease if you don't know what it is. You want a doctor to figure out what's wrong before handing you some medicine or cutting you open.

The same is true spiritually. If we're going to simplify our lives, we've got to make a proper diagnosis. A good doctor will ask how long you've had your symptoms, if certain diseases are common to your family, what your diet is like and how often you exercise, and on and on. I've found that two diagnostic questions are very helpful in getting to the root of this spiritual disease.[1]

> If we're going to simplify our lives, we've got to make a proper diagnosis.

Two Diagnostic Questions

The first question reveals what's behind the bigger, better, faster, more. If you keep running relentlessly toward an elusive goal, there's got to be something that motivates you, something behind the pressures and demands driving you. You'll go a long way toward finding out what it is by asking yourself this first question: *What do you want to be known for?*

Maybe you want to be known as a kind and loving person. Perhaps what you want to be known for has more to do with your role—being a great mom or dad or student. Or maybe your skills or abilities are the key; you want to be known as a problem solver or a wise person or for being great at your job. If you had to write down what you want to be known for, what would you write?

Most of us can come up with some pretty good goals. I don't know anyone who would say, "I want to be known for being an overextended, hurried parent who doesn't connect with my kids." Or, "I want to be a successful businessperson who is on my third marriage and doesn't have time for any deep friendships." We know the right answers.

But most of us have a disconnect between what we consciously acknowledge and what our time and energy are devoted to. We say one thing, but our schedules and to-do lists don't reflect our words. Intellectually we have one list of priorities while practically we demonstrate another.

The second question is a lot like the first, but it is more precise. *If you could only be remembered for one thing, what would it be?* If you had to describe your goal in just one word—not one sentence or phrase, but a single word—what would you say? I realize this isn't easy, but if you could only be remembered for one thing, what would it be? If your spouse or kids or friends described you, what one word would you most want to hear that epitomizes who you are?

Maybe you can think of several possible answers. But there's one word that should be at the top of the list. Every other attribute is at best a distant second. Your friends and family may think you're a wonderful person, but if you don't have this one characteristic, you're missing what matters most. The number one characteristic we need to embody, the highest priority for our lives, is LOVE!

There's nothing wrong with wanting to be a great spouse or parent, a good friend, an excellent artist, businessperson, counselor, athlete, or anything else. Being "creative" or "brilliant" or "successful" is not a bad goal. If we can fulfill all our desires for the roles we want to have and the things we want to accomplish, that's great. But above all, if we don't epitomize love, none of the rest matters.

That's the key to simplifying life: making love your number one priority. Yet most of what we do, no matter how good our intentions are, undermines our ability to love well. We clutter our lives with complications and crowd out the one thing that would simplify them. We find ourselves doing more and loving less. We need a practical game plan to focus on what matters most.

∾ QUESTIONS FOR
Reflection/Discussion ∾

- To what degree are you doing the Silicon Valley Shuffle? What does that dance look like where you live and in your personal life?

- What does your schedule indicate you want to be known for? Are you currently investing most of your time in the things you want to be remembered for? Why or why not?

- What is the biggest barrier to your slowing down and simplifying your life?

- Are there any relationships in your life that are being hindered by the things on your to-do list? Which ones?

- How, specifically, can you begin to be more loving this week? With whom? Why?

TWO

What's Love Got to Do with It?

I can remember driving in my car back in the eighties and singing along with Tina Turner: "What's Love Got to Do with It?" One of the catchiest songs I've ever heard. Whenever I hear it, it brings back memories. But you know how it is sometimes when you just sing along to something without really being conscious of the words. Sooner or later, you realize what you're singing.

I looked at the words of this song a little more closely, and found that it basically says love probably isn't true. It's just an ideal. It's a secondhand emotion, a sweet old-fashioned notion. And really, who needs a heart when a heart can be broken? Real love is too rare, too dangerous, too costly. In other words, Tina seems to have given up on love because she doesn't know what real love is.

So what's love got to do with simplifying your life? Well, everything. Love and simplicity go together. On the surface they may not seem to have an obvious connection—after all, love isn't always uncomplicated. But love does redirect our focus and priorities. Love unravels that complex, over-extended lifestyle that keeps us always running but never arriving.

One Overarching Principle

Our main Bible text in this book will be the apostle Paul's beautiful writing on love in 1 Corinthians 13. Paul's goal in this passage was to help the church of Corinth focus on what matters most. In helping them deal with misplaced priorities, he gives the Corinthians one over-arching principle as a guideline to help them determine what's really important. His guideline was simple, yet profound: *anything minus love is nothing*. If we can we learn to measure our activities, accomplishments, and relationships by this principle, our lives will get a lot less complicated. If this were a mathematical equation, God would be saying:

anything - love = nothing

Paul expressed it like this:

> *If I speak in the tongues of men or of angels, but do not have love, I am only a resounding gong or a clanging cymbal. If I have the gift of prophecy and can fathom all mysteries and all knowledge, and if I have a faith that can move mountains, but do not have love, I am nothing. If I give all I possess to the poor and give over my body to hardship that I may boast, but do not have love, I gain nothing.*
>
> (1 Corinthians 13:1–3 NIV)

Corinth was a bustling, influential city—possibly a lot like where you live—and the Christians there were busy exercising all kinds of spiritual gifts in their somewhat disorderly gatherings. Even though the Corinthian believers were zealous about faith, teaching, healing, prophecy, and many other godly activities, they had dysfunctional relationships. They were a very busy church—so much so that they had lost their focus.

That's why Paul gave them this overarching principle. They were doing a lot of good things, but they were doing them for the wrong reasons. We can be great at all we do and fulfill all our dreams, but if we do it without love, it's worth nothing. If we accumulate enough to give ourselves and our families a comfortable, privileged life, but don't have love, we've missed what matters. If we accomplish great things—even great things that advance God's kingdom—but don't have love, there's no value in it. Anything without love is nothing. In fact, God makes it clear that *everything* without love is nothing.

The main theme of 1 Corinthians, chapters 12–14 is spiritual maturity. Many people are familiar with chapter 13 as a stand-alone passage about love—maybe you've seen it on a plaque or heard it read at a wedding. But the primary reason for discussing gifts and love in the first place is to deal with the issue of spiritual maturity. What does it mean to be spiritual? How can chaotic lives be put back in order? What really matters most?

The Corinthians had some pretty strong opinions on that. Some believed that the gift of *speaking in unknown languages* was evidence of true spirituality. After all, no one could speak in tongues unless God's Spirit was in him, right? Others believed that *prophecy*—hearing from God and telling others what he said—was what made you spiritual. What could be more important than revealing God's truth to people? But apparently these things aren't enough.

In fact, Paul goes a lot further than saying they aren't enough—he actually says they are *nothing*. He says that even the noblest works are worthless if they aren't motivated by love. Look at all the spiritual activities and attitudes he specifically points out:

> Even the noblest works are worthless if they aren't motivated by love.

- ❧ speaking foreign languages by God's Spirit

- ❧ speaking the language of angels

- ❧ having a prophetic gift—hearing God's voice and declaring it to others

- ❧ understanding deep mysteries

- ❧ having great knowledge

- ❧ having great faith

- ❧ giving everything away to the poor

- ❧ dying as a martyr

Most of us would see that list as pretty impressive evidence of spiritual maturity. But what does Paul say it amounts to without love? Nothing. Not having love nullifies the benefit or the value of otherwise good attitudes and actions. Everything the Corinthians valued most amounted to *nothing* if love wasn't behind it.

That says a lot about the activities we fill our lives with. Why are we doing so much? Because we believe our lives will be better. We're convinced that earning a little more money by working a little harder will give us a little higher standard of living; that getting the kids involved in a few more activities will give them advantages in developing skills and building friendships; that doing more at church helps more people, makes us feel better about ourselves, and builds God's kingdom. And we're right—to a certain extent. All of these activities are genuinely good. But all of them can be done—or overdone—from wrong motives. If they aren't prompted by and filled with love, they are, in Paul's words, worthless. And if they take us away from simply loving those around us—in person, face-to-face—they steal from what's really important. Doing more does not equal loving more.

That's why we, like the Corinthians, can be busy with all kinds of good activities and still have lives filled with dysfunctional relationships. The Corinthians gossiped about one another, competed for attention, and were divided into factions. Their spiritual gifts, no matter how impressive, didn't solve their problems. Their ministry in the church didn't fix their home life. They weren't as spiritual as they thought they were. And when our lives are filled with lots of activity and little love, we aren't either.

Paul says there's a more excellent way.

Love's Supremacy

Maybe it would help us grasp what God is saying to us if we stepped back and looked at Paul's language from a psychological perspective. Note the progression he develops in verses 1–3:

- If I speak without love (*perform*) = It *produces* nothing!

- If I have many things without love (*possess*) = I *become* nothing!

- If I sacrificially give without love (*provide*) = It *profits* nothing!

The apostle is talking about our search for significance and the ways we try to achieve it. In today's language, it might be expressed like this:

- a *performance orientation*—I matter because of what I can do.

- a *materialistic orientation*—I matter because of what I possess.

- a *resource orientation*—I matter because of what I can provide.

All are dead-end streets when it comes to relationships. Note also the progression of futility: *provides nothing* ➙ *becomes nothing* ➙ *profits nothing.*

In other words, whatever you're doing with your time and your life, you're wasting it if you're not loving people.

So when love isn't our focus, our lives get bent out of shape. We can summarize the effects of these misplaced priorities in three ways:

Performing *in your world with the greatest gifts and abilities, but without love, produces nothing.* Some of us have learned to perform for strokes and affirmation, which feels great but is actually a cheap substitute for real love and deep relationships. Attention is not the same as love.

I wish you could meet a great group of friends called Prime Movers. It's a customized discipleship process for executives, business owners, and lovers of Christ who have achieved great personal and financial *success* in the first half of their lives and who long to achieve real *significance* and kingdom impact in the second half of their lives.

We meet in groups of six to eight people and share deeply and honestly. You would be shocked at their stories. Millionaires, pro-ball players, CEOs, and leaders from all backgrounds share the baggage that drove many of them to perform and seek the affirmation of others, only to experience the "emptiness of success" without love.

Possessing *the best, the finest, and the most amazing things you can imagine, but without love, amounts to nothing.* Paul was talking about spiritual gifts in 1 Corinthians, but the principle applies even more in a materialistic society like the United States. We have mental markers about what we drive, where we live, what title or position we have, where our kids go to school, and more. What we possess in terms of position and privilege—and the esteem we think comes with it—doesn't live up to its promise. People are driven by things as irrelevant as how quickly they move up the ladder or how far their kids can hit a ball. So they

> People are driven by things as irrelevant as how far their kids can hit a ball.

practically live in their SUV and eat fast food most nights as they go from practice to practice; or couples see each other briefly in the morning and then reconnect just before bedtime, only to start the cycle of fatigue all over again the next day. We know there has to be more, so we think we are only living like this "for a season," but the season never ends. The to-do list just gets longer, the kids' activities get more demanding, and one day we look back and realize that we've spent most of our lives chasing after the wind.

Sacrificially **providing** *for those you love, for the neediest people, or for the greatest cause on earth, but without love, profits nothing.* Most of us aren't trying to live at an insane pace. Most people tell me they've tried to slow down and just keep getting pulled back into the current. But in the process of trying to provide the best for yourself and your kids, now and in the future, you start to feel like you can never get out.

The result is that many of us live very hurried, over-extended, complex lives with shallow, superficial relationships, even with our closest friends and family members. We have unconsciously come to believe that *performing* well, *possessing* much, and *providing* stuff is what life is all about. We tie our value and significance to our performance and possessions rather than our relationships, and it shows. It isn't good for our souls, our marriages, our children, or our friendships.

A Prescription for Freedom

Enough diagnosis and evaluation, let's get to the solution. Let's admit it, most all of us are living too fast, doing too much, and loving too little. How can we cooperate with God's Holy Spirit in us and become the kind of loving people we all long to become? What's the key to transformation? I think the doctor would get his pad out and write down these three things:

Rx #1: The Secret to Simplifying Your Life Is Focus

Maybe that isn't earth-shattering news, but it's still true. We need to do less, but do it in a deeper, more relational way. Many of us have tried that and stuck with it—for a couple of days or maybe even a couple of weeks. But it only works when we consistently say yes to what matters most. This can be extraordinarily difficult unless we fully grasp Rx #2. We'll talk more about how to do this in the pages ahead.

Rx #2: You Can Only Do Less When You Choose to Love More

This has been the most helpful part of the cure for me. I've tried again and again to tweak my schedule. I read time-management books, I get up early in the morning, and I know how to multitask. Yet my activities seem to multiply until I've got way too many plates spinning. So tweaking my schedule isn't the answer. In order for the things that matter most to rise to the top of my list of priorities, I have to make a conscious decision to love more. Just saying no to some things on the to-do list doesn't work. I have to learn to say yes to things that matter more.

> Tweaking my schedule isn't the answer. I have to make a conscious decision to love more.

That really hit home when we found out Theresa had cancer. I've never said no to so many other things so quickly and easily as I did then. My top priority immediately became spending time with her and walking with her through the treatment. I'll talk more about that later, but I've had other glimpses of what's really important too. One of those perspective-shifting moments came when I took a trip to South Africa and Zimbabwe a couple years ago. I make it a habit to travel overseas at least once a year, but it had been a few years since I was able to do it. I had been keeping a hurried pace and had taken on new responsibilities, and I knew that if I didn't step back and regain some perspective, I'd just keep getting deeper into the bigger-better-faster-more lifestyle. So Theresa and I spent some time with South African pastors and then visited a ministry to orphans that we had been supporting. I knew that looking into the eyes of orphans who live in shacks would help me refocus.

We visited a home in Zimbabwe where about ten girls live with two older women. They get a good meal there, tend a garden, raise chickens, and learn the Bible. When we got out of the car, one of the girls came over to us wearing a bright smile. She was normally kind of shy, but she walked up to me and held her arms up. I picked her up and walked around with her on my hip for the next half hour. Her name was Blessing.

Then we talked with a thirteen-year-old girl who had been taken off the streets when she was five. A lot can happen to a four- or five-year-old orphan wandering the streets, and this girl had been through some really tough times. But now, after several years at the home, this articulate girl began talking about her relationship with Jesus and the people around her. She just beamed when she shared how much she was loved. And with Blessing on my hip and this girl who knew the love of God in front of me, I realized that these kids possessed what so many of us are chasing after. They aren't taking drugs to fall asleep at night. They don't have long to-do lists. They have very simple lives and are satisfied with their loving relationships with the people around them.

How did I have two weeks to go be with orphans and spend time with pastors ministering in difficult places? I said "no" to some things on my list of priorities and said "yes" to something that would cultivate my love. I came back feeling richer, fuller, and a lot less stressed about my life.

Rx #3: You Redefine Success When You Change the Questions

The third piece of this transformation puzzle is for us to redefine success. That isn't easy to do because we live in a culture that defines "success" in terms of achievements (and the recognition that goes along with them), wealth, status, beauty, and the right connections (not to be confused with real relationships) because that's what our culture most highly values. If we don't have a healthy bank account, a position of influence, an appealing appearance, or recognition for what we have accomplished—or at least two or three from that list—we don't feel successful. Even when we are rich in the things that matter—faith, unconditional love, a deep relationship with God and others—we tend to measure our "success" the way society does.

That has to change. For one thing, our definitions of success don't line up with God's. Shouldn't that be a little alarming? But even beyond that, our definitions of success lead us down some slippery slopes. In our attempts to *perform*, *possess*, and *provide*, we ask ourselves the wrong questions and then look to the people around us for affirming answers—a dynamic that plays out in some pretty unhealthy ways.

One of the things that has helped me the most is to identify three underlying questions that my life and time are asking and replace them with questions that love is asking. We begin to redefine success by changing the questions:

- From "How did I do?" to "Who am I becoming?"

- From "What do I have?" to "How am I using it?"

- From "How much do I give?" to "Why do I give it?"

You might consider writing the above questions on a three-by-five card and reading them over for the next few weeks. You'd be surprised at how much of our drive and hurried pace are rooted in the secret fears we all have in answering these questions. Let's explore how this works with all of us.

The first underlying question is "How did I do?" That's a performance question. It begins when we're children with parents, teachers, and coaches, and it translates into adulthood with bosses, board members, sales reports, and anyone or anything else that measures success. A much better question is "Who am I becoming?" That's a character question. It takes the focus off performance and puts it on the qualities we want to develop.

The second question we use to measure ourselves is "What do I have?" That emphasizes our possessions and stokes our drive to acquire more and more stuff. The better question is "How am I using what I have?" That puts the focus not on our possessions but on our stewardship.

The third question we usually ask to determine how successful we are is "How much do I give?" In other words, how am I providing for those around me? What sacrifices am I making to help others? Again, this question leads to a superficial answer and a false picture of what's really important. The better question is "Why do I give?" That moves our attention from the size of a sacrifice to its motive—a much more love-based issue.

With all three of these questions, we are shifting from measurable quantities that may or may not be good indicators to less tangible but more important qualities that really matter. In other words, we are taking our eyes off *performance*, *possessions*, and *provision* and putting them on character—especially love.

If Love Is the Answer, Then . . .

I don't think I've ever met anyone who said, "I want a more complex, overwhelming, demanding life." Hundreds, however, have told me that they desperately need to simplify, slow down, and get more focused—usually on God, relationships, marriage, or family. But that statement is almost always followed by this one: "But I don't know how. I've tried, but I always get sucked back in."

You'll notice that this prescription for freedom doesn't boil down to how to do less or how to say no. That's not what this is about. We've all tried that, and very few of us have been very successful at it. The secret is in learning, in Christ's power, to say "yes" to loving more.

But if the key is to love more, that raises some very important questions. If love is the answer, then we really need to know what healthy, biblical love looks like. What is love? How do we practice it? We'll start that journey in the next chapter, but take a minute and process the questions below first. Remember it's about learning to love, not how fast you finish this book. So linger. Ponder. Talk with God. Reflect. Enjoy the journey.

QUESTIONS FOR
Reflection/Discussion

- What's love got to do with simplifying your life?

- In what ways have you attempted to simplify your life in the past? What was your experience with those attempts?

- How can we discern whether we are motivated by love or by some other drive in our activities and relationships?

- If someone asked you to define success, what would you have said in the past? How has your lifestyle been a reflection of that definition? How would you define success now?

⤷ Have you been through experiences that shifted your perspective and suddenly rearranged your priorities? If so, what lasting effects did those experiences have? What practical steps can you take to live from a new perspective and make it last?

THREE

Love Is the Answer

What do England Dan and John Ford Coley have in common with the apostle Paul? All three are convinced that "Love Is the Answer!" Dan and Coley were pop artists from Texas who made the song famous in the seventies, and Paul wrote the most acclaimed piece of literature on love ever penned.

Even those who have never opened the Bible are probably familiar with the classic passage on love from 1 Corinthians 13 that we looked at in the last chapter. Unfortunately, most people think this is merely a beautiful description of "ideal love" to be engraved on plaques and read at weddings. Nothing could be further from the truth. These words were written to a church filled with disunity. Despite their many gifts and good works, their lack of love resulted in misplaced priorities, fractured relationships, and ongoing conflict. They were driven to perform, but they were missing the one ingredient that would have mattered most. Paul told them that love was the answer to their problems.

If love is the answer, it's really important to understand exactly what love is. The word is used in so many different ways in our language and culture that it can apply to anything from last night's dessert to a favorite hobby to a lifelong relationship with a spouse. If we're going to choose to love more, we really need to know what love looks like.

What love is not. Biblical love isn't an emotion. When we decide to love others better, we often equate love with a nice feeling that makes us happy, and then we try to muster up that feeling as often as we can. Love certainly may involve feelings at times, but it isn't based on them. It's a choice about how to treat other people, always seeking their good. It begins with those close to us—

> We don't have the power for this kind of love on our own, but God will give it to us.

roommate, spouse, family (including in-laws), friends—but extends all the ways to acquaintances and even enemies. We don't have the power for this kind of love on our own, but God will give it to us.

What love is. In 1 Corinthians 13, Paul doesn't even define love. He describes it. Though it makes a nice wedding verse or a living room plaque, these words were written for an altogether different purpose. This passage was meant to correct the busy, distorted, overextended, misdirected lives of the Corinthian Christians. So Paul gives them fifteen descriptions of love, each of which is directed at correcting some dysfunction in their present relationships. It's a very practical chapter on what love looks like.

That's what we're going to explore in the following pages—what it means to simplify our lives by doing less and loving more. As we choose to let these truths sink into our hearts and then into our actions, we'll find ourselves living with greater focus, less stress, deeper relationships, and more meaning.

Experience has taught us that when love is minimized, trivia is maximized. The important becomes trivial and the trivial becomes important. There is a palpable ache in people's hearts these days: they want to do life with people who really care and who will go deep with them. There is a longing to maximize love and minimize the trivial. As I pastor people today, I see a new desire for quality of life over quantity of activities. We are beginning to realize the two don't go hand in hand. Real, authentic love is the substance we're looking for.

So if love is the key to simplifying our lives, we are left with a really big question: How can we maximize love so it takes the highest priority in our lives and so the things that stress us out become less important and less demanding? The answer is learning how to love in real

> How can we maximize love so it takes the highest priority in our lives?

life. It can't be simply a motivational device that works about thirty seconds or thirty hours, depending on your personality. Loving in real life isn't about trying harder or platitudes about the importance of love or an emotional appeal. And it isn't theoretical—great-sounding principles that don't really work in real time. We need a practical, ground-level approach that changes our love from a noun to a verb in everyday life. That's what Paul gives us in 1 Corinthians 13. We'll discover that this chapter of scripture really is *the answer* to how to love well in real-life situations. Beginning here and continuing through the next few chapters, we'll ask and answer four questions based on 1 Corinthians 13. Let's start with question number one.

Question #1: How Does Love Respond to Hurts?

Love is patient, love is kind. (1 Corinthians 13:4)

Paul begins his description of love in verse 4: "Love is patient, love is kind." Remember, he's addressing busy, inwardly divided believers who have skewed priorities. There are all kinds of problems in this church—we'll discuss some of them as we go through this passage—and one of the biggest is how they treat one another. These first two descriptive words go straight to the problem of how they respond to hurts. How do you respond when someone hurts you?

We've all been hurt. You don't have to live very long to realize that pain is inevitable. And you don't have to be in the church very long to realize that Christians can hurt each other too. We're going to get hurt—in families, at church, among co-workers and acquaintances, anywhere. The potential is always there. It's impossible to relate to people with any real depth without getting hurt at some point. The question is how we choose to respond when

> It's impossible to relate to people with any real depth without getting hurt.

someone hurts us. Some of us want payback, and we'll get it by lashing out with words or by being passive-aggressive. Others respond by withdrawing and avoiding, or even just cutting off the relationship—that's how we protect ourselves from further pain. But if we can understand our hurts and, more importantly, the love that more than compensates for them, we can learn to love others.

When we're offended, it's usually because someone has threatened our drive to *perform*, *possess*, or *provide*. The wounds we receive from others hit us in the places where we most want to succeed—the reputation we work for or the achievements we crave. But what if we found our complete security in our identity in Christ? What if our drive to *perform*, *possess*, and *provide* was governed by the fact that we are already accepted, eternally rich, and fully equipped with what matters? What if we learned to focus on love and not on our image or activities? There would be very little left to defend. We would be almost unoffendable.

Think about how hard it is to carry around offenses—to hold a grudge or justify ourselves or feel a need for vindication. We can go through a lot of mental gymnastics to show that we've been misunderstood or to "pay back" a slight or an insult, even if only in our own minds. Offenses are a heavy burden to bear—and in light of the love we have been given, they are a completely unnecessary burden. If

we refuse to carry them, life becomes a lot less complicated. But how does this work? How does patience overcome our hurts and give love in return? The answer is in
understanding what God means when he calls us in love to
be "patient."

The word for patience is *makrothymeo*—from *macro*
(big, broad, spread out) and *thymos* (passion). So it's
"stretched-out passion." Some translations call it "longsuf-
fering," and here it refers not to being patient in tough circumstances but in dealing with people. That little remark
that hurts your feelings, that person who is difficult to deal
with, that invitation that everyone except you seemed to
get—anything that might cause you either to shut down
or to lash out. Love responds with patience. Our normal
reaction is to lash out in passion or anger. But patience is
allowing God to defuse anger. It's absorbing the blow of
hurt and rejection. Repeatedly. It doesn't default to natural or immediate reactions. It chooses to bear the offense
rather than retaliate.

Love is also *kind*. It responds with what the person who
wounded you least deserves: goodness, winsomeness, and
encouragement. Most of us don't react to offenses that way.
We might forgive, perhaps grudgingly and after some time,
but we don't normally try to figure out a way to affirm and
encourage the person who hurt us. But that's exactly what

the kindness of love does. It recognizes where most people's bad behavior flows from: they've been wounded themselves. Someone hurt them, so now, out of their insecurities, they inflict their pain on others, usually unintentionally. Instead of adding to those wounds with a harsh response, our love offers healing words or actions instead.

Let me share a word picture for this—a figurative, mental image that portrays the attitudes of patience and kindness.[2] Imagine absorbing blows like a pillow and then responding to the offense with a hug. That's what patience (absorbing blows) and kindness (giving hugs) looks like. Of course there are times when we need to have some boundaries. There are situations in which a long history of abuse or a pattern of painful interaction requires a wise response. Patience and kindness don't require us to submit to repeated, damaging interaction. But those exceptions aside, can you imagine what would happen in your everyday relationships at home and work if you absorbed blows like a pillow and returned kindness instead? How many little spats, arguments, and wounded hearts would be eliminated if you consciously asked God to help you respond to hurt with love this week? You will be amazed to see tension and conflict no longer escalating but dissolving as you absorb the blow and give a hug after someone hurts you.

That's what Jesus did, isn't it? When he was on the cross—betrayed, rejected, brutally beaten—he absorbed the blow. He committed himself to God, forgave those who were executing him, and then, after he rose, forgave those who had abandoned and rejected him. Why? Because love has no agenda to retaliate or punish. It is free to treat people in a way that's best for them.

> Love is free to treat people in a way that's best for them.

When Theresa and I were in South Africa, we met a Christian woman who was one of Nelson Mandela's secret service people. Mandela spent more than twenty years in prison thinking about the injustice he had experienced personally and that other South Africans had experienced under apartheid. It would have been normal for years of prison to produce a bitter man ready to take revenge. In fact, when Mandela became president, whites fled the country by the thousands, assuming that would be the case. Yet this white woman shared with me what it was like to work with him. He refused to have all black bodyguards. He refused to pay back evil for evil. He absorbed the blow and gave a hug. He demanded that the white people who had enforced apartheid be treated mercifully and kindly. That was his answer to the wounds his country had experienced. That's love. It took courage and strength, but Mandela's example and leadership resulted in a revolution without bloodshed.

Do you see how that response makes life a lot simpler than carrying offenses and figuring out how to retaliate? Conflict can be exhausting, but it isn't if we refuse to engage in it. Love makes relationships a lot less complicated and a lot more rewarding. It takes the focus off what we have, what we do, and who we are; and puts it on maintaining a connection and doing what's best for others. It's powerfully liberating.

> Conflict can be exhausting, but it isn't if we refuse to engage in it.

This kind of love is beyond our strength to give. In fact, we can't really give it unless we've experienced it. But when we realize that God doesn't relate to us on the basis of our *performance*, *possessions*, or *provision*—and that he is unimaginably patient and kind toward us—we find his kind of love flowing naturally from our lives to others. When his love really sinks in, we are empowered to give it freely.

So if you want this kind of love to really sink in, your first assignment isn't to go out and try to be more patient and kind. The first step is to let God be patient and kind to you. In the words of 1 John 4:19, "We love because he first loved us." In other words, our ability to love him and others flows out of our experience of being loved by him.

Trying to express God's love to others without first knowing his love for us is like trying to be a fountain without a water source. We can't give what we don't have. Some of us beat ourselves up whenever we make a mistake, and we go through life feeling like we're always falling short. That's self-condemnation, and it destroys our ability to love. So let God love you extravagantly—be reminded that he is patient with your mistakes, your failures, and your sin. Thank him for his patience and kindness in your own life, and then notice how you begin to love others with the patience and kindness he has shown you.

❧ QUESTIONS FOR
Reflection/Discussion ❧

- ❧ What hurt comes to your mind that seems impossible to forgive?

- ❧ How do bitterness and unresolved conflict drain your energy?

- ❧ Can you think of a time you were patient (absorbing like a pillow) and kind (returning a hug) when someone hurt you? What were the results of your patience and kindness? How did the other person react?

🍃 When have you been in a conflict that escalated because no one was being patient or kind? How do you think the situation would have changed if authentic love had been expressed by one of the people involved?

🍃 How do stress, hurry, and multiple demands impact our patience with others?

🍃 How comforting is it to know God is patient with you? What are some evidences of his kindness toward you in the last week, month, or year?

🍃 Read the following quote each night at bedtime and make it your prayer each morning this week as your first step to simplifying your life.

Dear God,

When someone hurts my feelings, offends me, treats me in a way that causes me to feel rejected or angry, please help me by your Spirit's power to "absorb the blow" like a giant pillow and "return a hug" of kindness and affirmation to the very one who did it. Why? Because "love is patient, love is kind."

;

FOUR

Love Me Tender

Elvis Presley performed "Love Me Tender" on *The Ed Sullivan Show* on September 9, 1956, shortly before the single's release and about a month before the movie's release. On the following day, RCA received one million advance orders, making it a gold record before it was even released.

The king of rock and roll hit a raw nerve with this song that went beyond his personal charisma. The words speak of belonging, permanence, and acceptance until the end of time. These words are not uncommon in love songs, but the repeated refrain—actually a request to "love me tenderly"—reveals our inherent fear that our differences will drive us apart. As we continue our journey toward spiritual simplicity, the apostle Paul teaches us how love responds to those differences.

Question #2: How Does Love Respond to Differences?

ꙩ

It does not envy, it does not boast, it is not proud. It is not rude, it is not self-seeking, it is not easily angered, it keeps no record of wrongs. (1 Corinthians 13:4–5)

It's often said that differences are what attract a couple to each other, and differences are what drives them apart. That's true not only in romance but also in friendships and other relationships. The fact that God created everyone to be different makes this world interesting—we appreciate those with different personalities, different backgrounds, and different gifts and talents. But those differences can also make for a lot of tension, can't they? They can make love quite a challenge.

Paul addressed a lot of relational dysfunction in the Corinthians' fellowship, much of which was related to divisions among them. A survey of 1 Corinthians reveals very specific issues that Paul was correcting:

- Chapter 3: He rebukes them for envying one another.

- Chapters 4–5: He rebukes them for boasting and pride.

- Chapter 6: He accuses them of being self-centered in their arguments and lawsuits.

- Chapter 11: He rebukes them for being rude in the way they were taking the Lord's Supper.

- Chapter 12: He begins to make the case that love isn't behind any of these attitudes and behaviors. He explains how love works, using the illustration of a human body in which all parts function together out of necessity. With the parts of the body, differences are necessary and worth celebrating. Every part is important to the whole. In the diversity, there's unity.

Love Celebrates Differences

Paul carries out the metaphor of the body to show the absurdity of Christians comparing themselves to one another. If every part of the body were an eye, how would we be able to hear? If we had four hands and no feet, how would we be able to walk? Every part needs all the other parts. The head can't do without the feet, the eyes can't do without the hands, and so on. The important thing is how the body functions, not how much prestige each individual part has. God has arranged all the parts "just where he wanted them to be" (12:18). They are all vital.

To apply this picture spiritually means that all kinds of people belong in the church. They are part of something bigger and more important—the body of Christ. Different backgrounds, different levels of experience, different roles all contribute to the overall mission and purpose of the body. We may have different gifts, but from God's perspective, we don't have varying degrees of value or usefulness. We are made to be interdependent. We are designed to need one another, not be in competition with one another. Our value is equal in the eyes of God. The Corinthian church—as well as many churches today—was divided and cliquish. Paul's response is to tell them how ridiculous it is, in light of God's arranging of the parts, to compare themselves to one another.

That's the context that sets up chapter 13. Love doesn't envy, it doesn't boast, it isn't proud, and it doesn't keep a record of

Real love celebrates our differences!

wrongs. That isn't how love responds to differences. In fact, real love celebrates our differences!

The Corinthian church isn't all that unique. Its backbiting, gossiping, arguing tendencies are played out again and again today in families, organizations, and even churches. We aren't any different from the people of New Testament times in how we let healthy differences evolve into unhealthy divisions. We need to learn how to love just as much as they did.

It is amazing how our cultural background can unconsciously lead us to be inwardly critical of people we don't even know. When I pastored in a small rural town in Texas, I found myself inwardly judgmental of how people dressed, the kind of music they liked, and the "narrow" view of the world I perceived small-town people possessed. Eight years later, I left that town realizing they taught me how to be a pastor and that my external, judgmental viewpoints were a result of my own arrogance and ignorance. The depth and quality of their lives and relationships with Jesus prepared me for the next twenty years of ministry.

If we're going to learn how to love in real life, we'll have to learn how to respond to people with different personalities, different backgrounds, and different gifts. The bitterness and resentment that can spring up out of conflict have an enormous capacity to destroy and complicate our lives. Divisions and the hard feelings that come out of them are heavy burdens to bear and take up a lot of time and mental energy as we try to deal with them. Love unravels that complexity and releases the stress. Love doesn't have to figure out all of the dynamics of a conflict or the perfect response to it. It simply lets differences play out. It even celebrates and honors those differences by looking at ourselves and others as different pieces of a puzzle that have different colors and shapes and purposes but that fit together in a really beautiful way.

Comparison Always Leads to Carnality

> Until we really understand that we're purposefully unique, we'll have a tendency to compare ourselves with others.

Until we really understand that we're purposefully unique—fearfully and wonderfully made—we'll have a tendency to compare ourselves with others. And the results of comparing are never good. It always leads to carnality. The moment we compare our own gifts or position with someone else, sinful thoughts are produced: our singleness in light of their marriage, our income in light of theirs, our usefulness in God's kingdom in light of their fruitfulness. Either we see ourselves as inferior, in which case we become envious; or we see ourselves as superior, in which case we become arrogant.

We all struggle with envy and arrogance, but each of us tends habitually to fall into one camp more often than the other. So it's really helpful to recognize which one gives us the most trouble. Our perspective on differences can either create division in our relationships or create strength. Celebrating differences cultivates love. Using them to compare kills it.

Comparing ourselves with others and deciding that we are in some way inferior—that we come up short or got the raw end of the deal when God handed out gifts and blessings—may look like humility at times but actually leads to bitterness and resentment. And comparing ourselves and deciding that we are in some way superior—that we are more highly favored or more inherently valuable—is arrogance. These attitudes are two sides of the same coin. "Love does not envy, it does not boast" (1 Corinthians 13:4). Envy and boasting are sinful responses to our bitterness.

Paul identified these two major responses to the differences among people and then described some of their fruit.

Envy and pride result in dishonoring, self-seeking, angry, judgmental attitudes and actions. Comparison always leads to ungodly, spiritually immature results.

Comparing Upward: Envy

Envy compares upward and produces jealousy, anger, resentment, and bitterness. The Hebrew word in Old Testament passages has connotations of ever increasing heat—an emotion that burns inside. It's like a foot looking at the hand and saying, "That's not fair! I have to deal with dust and dirt, and the hand gets expensive rings and nail polish put on it. I'm all guts and no glory, while the hand gets to play instruments, create art, and do surgery."

> It's the you're-important-and-I'm-a-nobody syndrome, and it isn't pretty. Or true.

It's the you're-important-and-I'm-a-nobody syndrome, and it isn't pretty. Or true.

There's no limit to how that plays out in our lives. You've been praying for a promotion, but somebody with less experience, fewer skills, and more connections lands the job. You've wanted to be married for years, but you're on your fourth roommate because the first three came home after dates and said, "He proposed! I'm getting married!" You've spent all your money trying—unsuccessfully—to have a baby, while every other couple in your Bible study group seems to get pregnant every time the weather changes. Your response to these things on the outside is usually something like, "Oh, that's wonderful. Congratulations!" On the inside, the temptation to cry out, "That's not fair!" is almost irresistible.

Usually our unfulfilled desires are not wrong. There's nothing selfish or ungodly about wanting a promotion, a marriage, a baby, or anything else we normally hope for. The problem is in thinking that we might matter more or be more complete if God would only do what we're expecting him to do. That's really what's at the heart of envy—a belief that we would matter, that our hearts would be complete, "if only . . ." So when God doesn't fulfill that expectation, or when he delays longer than we would like, we develop a sense of unfairness about it. "If he really loved me, I wouldn't still be single." "If he was really taking care of me, I wouldn't have lost all that money when the recession hit." "If he really cared about the desires of my heart, we would have several children by now." "I went to school

> At the heart of envy is a belief that we would matter, that our hearts would be complete, "if only . . ."

with that guy, and we started our careers together, but his has taken off and mine has stagnated. God must have better plans for him."

The root of these thoughts is the idea that God isn't really good, that maybe he's holding out on us, but somehow he isn't holding out on others. He must be more pleased with them—and, well, maybe we aren't as important or as needed as we thought. It starts as a feeling, but then it moves to a pattern inside the heart. We feel "less than."

This is actually a lifelong battle, perhaps the greatest spiritual battle we will ever face. The temptation to mistrust God's goodness was behind the first temptation in Eden, and it's somewhere in the rationale behind every sin we commit. After all, if God isn't good—not just at a theological level, but in real, practical terms in our lives—then we may have to take matters into our own hands. We have to strive for our own security or arrange our own future because he might not, at least not the way we want him to. And then when things don't work out, all of our mistrust seems to be confirmed. God may be good theoretically, we rationalize, but in a mysterious way, his goodness doesn't apply to our lives. We

> We start to wonder if God can be trusted with any of our heart's true desires.

start to wonder if God can be trusted with any of our heart's true desires.

Envy springs up from such bitter roots, and it causes us to express resentment toward people who have really done nothing to deserve our resentment. Consciously or unconsciously, we usually distance ourselves from those we envy. Seeing them enjoying the privileges and pleasures we want to experience is too painful, and it makes us feel less worthy. No one wants to subject themselves to situations that stoke those feelings, so our envy alienates us from others. Sometimes our resentment leaks out, and sometimes it simply removes us from the relationship. Either way, it isn't conducive to love.

We usually don't talk about these feelings. We don't ask people to pray for our envy problem. We inwardly beat ourselves up for our desires and disappointments, as if they are somehow sinful. But the word for envy actually means "to eagerly desire," and it isn't always used negatively in scripture. In 1 Corinthians 12:31 and 14:1, Paul uses the same word to encourage people to seek spiritual gifts. Eagerly desire them. Covet them. Be zealous for them. The word can either mean to be zealous or to be jealous. The difference is in the object of desire. It isn't always a problem.

Say, for example, you want—even eagerly desire—a bigger house. If you have the gift of hospitality and your motive is to love and serve more people, that's a zealous desire to honor God. But if your desire for a bigger house is to keep up with everyone else who is getting a bigger house, and you're embarrassed to keep inviting people over to your small house, and if you secretly believe the bigger house communicates that you've arrived . . . well, that's envy. If your desire is to have more so you will matter more, that's jealousy, and it can really complicate and stress out your life. If your desire is to honor God and minister more deeply, that's zeal motivated by love.

We need to redirect our desires, not kill them. There's nothing wrong with wanting to be married, have kids, get a promotion, or earn a better living. Those are honest, God-given desires. But the moment we begin to compare ourselves to others, we stop loving.

> We need to redirect our desires, not kill them.

The antidote for envy is to believe that God is good and is sovereign over the gifts and opportunities he has given us—and that in his wisdom he has been just as intentional in the lives of others. Trying harder not to envy won't work. We have to learn to think differently. We need to know deep down in our hearts that God is for us, that he wants to work in our lives, and that even when things don't seem to be going in the right direction, he cares and has a good plan.

I generally have more of a problem with arrogance than with envy—most people gravitate toward one or the other—but I had a bout with envy recently that surprised me. It involved a pastor friend in another state. Though we are similar in age and experience, his name suddenly seemed to be popping up at conferences and events everywhere, his books were showing up prominently in bookstores and catalogs, and people really seemed to be noticing his insights. Part of me was rejoicing that he was doing well and that the kingdom was growing through his ministry. And part of me was not nearly so positive. I felt "less than" and resentful, wishing that God would use my ministry and books that way.

After I struggled with envy for a while, God led me to take some very specific steps to deal with it. *First*, I faced it. I had rationalized my reaction lots of other ways, but it helped just to be honest and say I was jealous.

Second, I didn't try to get rid of my sincere desire for God to expand my influence and use my books. There's nothing wrong with wanting God to use my life for his glory. So I redirected my desire for God to use my life in the same way he was using my friend's and simply asked him to use me at whatever level he desired in order to build his kingdom—not in comparison to anyone else, but just however he wanted.

Third, I meditated on God's goodness. Whenever we question God's goodness, there's a lie somewhere in our thinking. It usually goes like this: "If God really cared, he would ————," and we tend to fill in the blank with things like giving us more opportunities, healing our bodies, blessing our finances, causing our kids to turn out like we hoped, and so on. So I refused to use that reasoning. Questioning his goodness was the first temptation in the Bible, and resisting it becomes a lifelong battle. God *is* good, and he longs to be generous. In his wisdom, he is working sovereignly to bestow his goodness in more ways than I can see. If I reflect on his goodness, I begin to see it at deeper and deeper levels.

Fourth, in order to overcome envy, we need to choose gratitude. We will either envy what other people have or thank God for what we have, not both. We can't hold jealousy and gratitude in the same heart. I began to thank God for all the ways he has used me, and I thanked him for the pastor I was envious of. As soon as I began to praise God and thank him for this man and his ministry, especially his impact on my life and on one of my sons, the envy began to dissipate.

> In order to overcome envy, we need to choose gratitude.

Finally, it's always helpful to try to connect with the people we're comparing ourselves to and serve them, if appropriate. I began praying for this man and wrote him an e-mail telling him how I'd noticed that God had been using him in some amazing ways. I thanked him for his impact in my life and encouraged him to keep pressing ahead. A few hours later, he e-mailed back with a "thanks," and that was that. I was free.

If we don't let go of envy and choose love, we will forever be running to keep up with those who make us feel inferior. That's a tiring, misguided way to live. Envy is one of those subtle attitudes that keeps us busier than we need to be. It's much better to realize that we're all part of the same body, each part performing a necessary function. We can stop comparing and rejoice in one another's contributions without being envious. That's exactly what love does.

Comparing Downward: Arrogance

The pufferfish is a relatively small fish, but it fills itself with water and becomes enormous when it feels threatened. It increases its own size in order to intimidate any potential predators. That's a lot like what we do when we compare ourselves to others. Sometimes we puff ourselves up out of insecurity, other times simply to let others know how important we are. Either way, it's a form of arrogance.

In contrast to comparing upwardly and feeling envious, we become proud—literally "puffed up, inflated, overvalued"—when we compare ourselves to others and think we're superior. In order to live up to this image, we either project our importance by puffing up (name-dropping, working our accomplishments into the conversation, etc.) or by tearing others down.

I have a theory that if you were to go into any coffee shop and listen in on the conversations, you would find that about four out of every five conversations involve two people talking about someone who isn't there, and the talk isn't positive. It's about what this person did or didn't do, how they don't measure up, and so on. There's something sadistically satisfying about putting others down because it makes us feel better about ourselves.

> There's something sadistically satisfying about putting others down because it makes us feel better about ourselves.

Think of all the ways pride complicates our lives. It's hard to maintain a sense of superiority. We always have to jockey for position, present the right image, back up our words with at least some evidence that supports them, demonstrate our value and importance if anyone ever happens to question it, and associate with people who help us feel better about ourselves. Most of that posturing is usually subconscious—we often aren't even aware we're doing it—but it's still exhausting. It fuels our pursuit of success in very unhealthy ways.

While the underlying assumption of the envious is "*I* don't matter, *I* don't measure up," the underlying assumption of the arrogant is "*You* don't matter, *you* don't measure up." We begin to feel entitled. We have a need to be the center of attention. We're special, after all. We need to be the go-to people for every important job because no one else can do the job as well. We start to feel like we don't need others as much as we used to, and so we become more independent. And in the process, we become indifferent to the needs of others because we're so preoccupied with ourselves.

When we develop that sense of independence, we also become more unaccountable to others. "Sure, there may be rules about money or sexual purity or integrity, but that's for other people in normal circumstances. But my schedule and the demands on my life are different. There are exceptions to the normal rules, and my situation happens to warrant those exceptions." That's where the independent, unaccountable mind tends to go, and at that point, the journey toward a downfall is usually a pretty quick one. As Proverbs 16:18 tells us, pride goes before a fall. Eventually the whole illusion begins to collapse.

The Bible and history are filled with people who started out in humility and trust and, after doing great things or becoming great leaders, ended up proud and independent. The more gifts, talents, power, and blessings we have, the greater the temptation hubris becomes. And the more our drive for affirmation has to be fed.

I was speaking to a group of business owners recently and challenged them to think about their lack of close friendships. People in their position don't have many genuine friends because they can fire or disinherit practically everyone around them. They are intimidating to those around them, which means they have a hard time developing close relationships. In addition, their wealth and power have attracted pseudo friends. They always wonder if the person befriending them is trying to get into their wallet or their network. So they become more untrusting, more independent, and less accountable. Over time they manipulate people to get things done. Pretty soon, they don't get much real love. All they get is affirmation. Affirmation rewards what we do; love accepts and rewards who we are. Like a drug addict seeking a "fix," they keep up the insane pace to earn strokes with their performance.

In order to break out of this misdirected attitude, arrogant people need to choose to be vulnerable in order to receive God's goodness. A few simple reminders can help bring us back to the right perspective.

> Arrogant people need to choose to be vulnerable in order to receive God's goodness.

First, we need to remember that everything we have comes from God. "What do you have that you did not receive?" Paul asks in 4:7. Everything we've been given—our natural talents and abilities, our opportunities to acquire learning and develop skills, our spiritual gifts, and even our own lives—has come from God. We didn't choose where we came from, what families we were born into, or what privileges we were given. We may have chosen to work hard and take advantage of opportunities, but even being in a position to do so was granted by God. Everything comes from him. He can lift us up or bring us down. We have stewardship over our positions and possessions, not ownership.

Second, we need to remember our roots. Most of us with a high position or many possessions have come out of more humble times. If we look back over our lives, we can see how God has taken us from one point to another to another, providing for us and giving us opportunities to get where we are now. And the truth is God does the same for everyone we compare ourselves with. We don't know the future of the people we meet. God's purposes for them are as significant as his purposes for us, no matter how their lives look to us. Remembering where we came from—and recognizing where others may be going—will give us a humble perspective.

Third, it helps to spend time with people who know our roots. They won't be swayed by our current position or influence. No matter what is ever said or written about us, no matter how many titles or degrees we receive, they won't be impressed. They will love us for who we are, be honest with us about what they see, and demonstrate love in a way we won't get from many others. I have a close friend named A.C. who has known me for more than thirty years. He was there in my first pastorate of thirty-five people in that small rural town in Texas. We were recently traveling together and discussing an opportunity to speak to one hundred CEOs in Korea and partner with two churches in Hong Kong, when he stopped and said, "You've come a long way from those early days, Chip." Then he added a word of warning: "Never forget your roots." Genuine friends will remind us that no matter where we are now, God is the one who got us there.

And finally, if we struggle with arrogance, it's important to admit our need and invite people deeper into relationship with us. More than a few times I've been reminded, at the end of a day, of incidents throughout the day when I acted insensitively, when I postured to impress someone, when I pretended to be busy so I wouldn't have to deal with someone, and when I displayed other ugly examples of pride. My guess is that you can remember moments like that too. If we confess those tendencies, admit our need for meaningful relationships, and then open ourselves up to loving others around us, the comparisons will subside, and pride will become much less of a problem.

As I've said, we all tend to lean toward one side or the other in this tension between envy and arrogance. Some of our tendencies come from the personality we were born with, some come from our giftedness in certain areas, and some come from our upbringing. I mentioned a case of envy earlier, but my greater temptation is arrogance. My dad was determined to teach me to read when I was three years old. He'd have me stand up in front of people and read short sentences, or gather a crowd and have me spell things like "intercontinental ballistic missiles" out loud. It was pretty impressive for a three-year-old. "Chip," he would say, "this country's going to need a good president one day." I think he was trying to groom me for greatness. The good side of this is that I grew up with a lot of confidence. The bad side is that . . . well, I grew up with a lot of confidence. Maybe too much. So I've struggled with an arrogant attitude that God has been patiently and consistently addressing for years.

Other people have huge struggles with envy. They never feel like they measure up. "Why did God make her so pretty?" "How did he get that kind of job?" "Why do I have to bat eighth in the lineup?" And the more they look at the successes of others, the more they feel that they are failures.

The remedy is to have a sober self-assessment and an accurate view of God.[3] Trying harder doesn't help. No envious person is going to get rid of his or her envy just by trying not to have it. The key is to focus on God—to believe that he's good and that he's in control. Even if everything in this season doesn't look great for you, there are other seasons coming. He has a unique plan for each of us that fits what we were made to do and correspondingly brings us the greatest joy. We mistakenly compare our weaknesses with others' strengths to our own peril. And he made you, cares for you, and is watching over every detail of your life. That's what matters.

> The remedy is to have a sober self-assessment and an accurate view of God.

One of the greatest ways to deal with envy and arrogance is to meditate on what God thinks of you. He is completely enamored with his people—full of love for his sons and daughters. Nothing we ever do will cause him to love us more, and nothing we do can ever cause him to love us less. He already values us far more than we can imagine. That takes care of our envy. In fact, if we really knew how much he values us, it might cause us to become puffed up—except for the fact that he values *all* of his children that much. So whether we're looking at ourselves or our neighbor, we're seeing someone who is treasured beyond words. There's no room for feeling "less than" when we know how much God adores us, but there's also no room for "greater than" when we know how much he adores others. There's just balance—and a lot of opportunities for healthy, authentic love.

In this chapter, we've seen how love responds when relationships feel threatening—when we've been wounded by others or feel insecure about our position relative to others. But how does love respond when relationships feel threatening to those around us? One of love's greatest challenges is failure, but it's also one of love's greatest opportunities. In the next chapter, we will learn how love responds to failure.

∼ QUESTIONS FOR
Reflection/Discussion ∼

- How do you tend to compare yourself with others? Do you gravitate more toward an upward comparison (envy) or a downward comparison (arrogance)? Do you tend to have too little self-esteem or too much?

- Which attitude bothers you more when you see it in other people—envy or arrogance? Why?

- Read Romans 12:3. How does this verse relate to the issues in this chapter?

- Why is it important to know what God thinks of us? How does his view give us a perfectly balanced perspective?

Resources for a sober self-assessment:
   www.LivingontheEdge.org/r12online

Read section 3 of *Living on the Edge,* "How to Come to Grips with the Real You."

FIVE

Looking for Love in All the Wrong Places

When Johnny Lee first heard the song "Lookin' for Love in All the Wrong Places," he felt as if he could have written it himself because it was the story of his life. He was a guy who, like the rest of us, just wanted to be loved, feel connected with others, and have meaning and purpose in his life; but he had made some big mistakes while looking for those things. When John Travolta first heard the song, he said it was the story of his life too. So when Lee recorded the song and Travolta acted it out in *Urban Cowboy*, the song rose to the top of the charts. Why? Because, like Lee and Travolta, millions of people felt like it was the story of their lives.

This song resonates with so many people because we're all looking for love—we crave intimacy and acceptance—

but we frequently search for it in the wrong places. It's your story, my story, and virtually everyone's story. We try to find a good thing in bad ways. But when we seek fulfillment in things that won't fulfill, we usually end up hurting ourselves and a few other people along the way. Our search can actually destroy our relationships, particularly when we step outside of God's will in the process. We can do a lot of damage if we don't know where to look for love.

Everyone fails. That's a fact. It's also a fact that we all have legitimate needs and desires that God wants us to pursue—for love, significance, security, and purpose, for example. Those two facts are connected by a third one: many of our failures come from our attempts to fulfill legitimate needs and desires in the wrong way. There's nothing wrong with wanting to be significant, to be loved, to give love, to feel secure, to have purpose, or to make an impact. God created us with these desires and wants us to pursue them. But often what looks fulfilling in these areas really isn't. In other words, we're looking for love in all the wrong places, and it hurts.

> Many of our failures come from our attempts to fulfill legitimate needs and desires in the wrong way.

Think about that. Often when someone hurts us or we

hurt someone else, it's because we were seeking something good. Our desire to accomplish something of significance, for example, turns into a desperate need to prove our significance. Our desire to connect and find intimacy morphs into a tendency to exploit the people around us for our own needs. Our desire for a relationship with God turns into a system of religious practices that never quite satisfy. All of these are legitimate needs placed in us by God, yet all of them seem to have a limitless capacity to be distorted. These are the things that complicate our lives and keep us running at a frantic pace in directions that never fulfill. And that misdirected pursuit is responsible for most of our failures. Thankfully, when we see those patterns, we can gain significant insight into how to avoid them.

What would happen if we could begin to see some of the patterns in our lives for what they are? What if we were able to recognize where we've blown it and had relationship breakdowns and could then redirect those God-given desires in healthy directions? We would be able to deal with our failures, and we would also be able to respond in love to the failures of others.

> We would be able to deal with our failures, and we would also be able to respond in love to the failures of others.

In his letter to the Corinthians, Paul outlines a number of ways the Christians in that church were looking for love and acceptance in the wrong places. The era of history and the culture have changed, but the patterns haven't. These apply just as much to us today as they did then.

- We seek acceptance and belonging by forming cliques and criticizing and excluding others, causing division. (1 Corinthians 3)

- We seek connection and intimacy through illicit sex, pornography, and emotional affairs that destroy marriages and ruin families. (1 Corinthians 5)

- We seek security and significance by obsessively trying to earn more and more money, even at the expense of our relationships. (1 Corinthians 6)

- We seek purity and holiness in our relationship with God by adopting legalistic standards and judging others' actions and motives, creating division in our fellowship. (1 Corinthians 8)

☜ We seek legitimate, godly pleasures but exercise our freedom in a way that becomes a stumbling block for those weaker in their faith. We allow our freedom to undermine their faith. (1 Corinthians 8)

In each of these cases, the desires are perfectly legitimate but the means employed to fulfill them are not. We're living examples of Johnny Lee's hit song. So many times, our gravest failures are attempts to look for love in all the wrong places, which leads us to the next major question in learning to love in real-life situations.

> The desires are perfectly legitimate but the means employed to fulfill them are not.

Question #3: How Does Love Respond to Failure?

Love does not delight in evil but rejoices with the truth. It always protects, always trusts, always hopes, always perseveres. (1 Corinthians 13:6–8)

Reality shows are like a petri dish for dysfunctional relationships. TV shows used to have writers and plots and professional actors, but now many of them put a bunch of incompatible and relationship-impaired people in the same house and see how long it takes for them to turn against one another. Or they set up ten single guys in a competition to win the affection of one gorgeous girl. These guys are good-looking, seem to be intelligent, and have decent jobs, but somehow they have so little dignity that they are willing to be just a guy in the rotation—the girl's "one and only" for a couple of hours until she's ready to move on to the next one. The main business of reality show contestants seems to be to stir up controversy with one another, and the worst in human nature is bound to come out. Rivalry, deception, manipulation, backbiting, anger, and jealousy take center stage. It's the relational equivalent of a twelve-car pileup on the interstate. You don't want to look, but you can't help looking.

According to ratings, people love these shows. For some reason, they are entertaining to us. We get some kind of perverted pleasure out of watching others mess up. Maybe it's because they make our mess-ups seem minor by comparison. We may have issues, but we don't have *those* issues—or that many. We can sit on our couches and watch people self-destruct in their relationships and make fools of one another—and themselves—without having to get involved. And it can be very satisfying to see people get exactly what their behavior deserves.

This is how tabloids make so much money on scandals. People fail very publicly, and plenty of us want to watch. Occasionally we might see a news story about a celebrity who's doing a lot for inner-city children or who is helping orphans in Africa, but much more often it's about who's in jail again or who's back in rehab. News stories about high-profile politicians, athletes, and entertainers being charged with a crime send ratings through the roof. Something in us finds bad behavior entertaining. But that's not love.

> Something in us finds bad behavior entertaining.
> But that's not love.

Love Responds to Failure with Truth and Grace

When we find delight in things that celebrate discord and dysfunction—things that don't bring health and life and restoration—we set ourselves up for broken, painful, and negative relationships.

Love responds to failure with truth and grace, not with fascination and satisfaction that so-and-so finally got what was coming to him. By responding in truth, love doesn't deny real problems. In fact, love demands truth. It doesn't settle for less. There's no sweeping things under the rug, at least not in the sense of refusing to face significant issues. Love without truth becomes mushy sentimentalism—the feel-good kind of love you get in a romance novel. But a good feeling doesn't help somebody with an addiction problem or destructive behaviors. That's not love. So love has to be filled with truth.

But by responding in grace as well as truth, love doesn't condemn someone for their problems or make those problems worse by bringing unnecessary attention to them. Love doesn't rejoice or find any satisfaction in things that don't fit God's design for our lives. It refuses to enjoy someone else's sin, misfortune, dysfunction, or pain. It's compassionate enough to tell the hard truth, but it does so with a heart of grace. Love confronts evil—but only because it has to. And the aim is always to restore.

This is to be our balanced response to failure. If the response is all truth and no grace, it comes across as legalistic and self-righteous—very judgmental. If it's all grace and no truth, it ends up being mushy emotionalism. The first extreme condemns and alienates a person, the second further enables that person's behavior. Truth or grace out of balance may be motivated by loving intentions, but it doesn't have a loving result. Only the balance can deal with a wrong behavior while affirming the person's value.

$$truth - grace = judgmentalism$$

$$grace - truth = sentimentalism$$

$$truth + grace = love$$

After giving us the overarching principle that love demands truth and rejoices in it, and that it refuses to rejoice in evil, Paul gives us four specific ways to respond to one another's failures: to protect, trust, hope, and persevere. Or, as some other translations put it, we are to bear all things, believe all things, hope all things, and endure all things.

Paul gives us four specific ways to respond to one another's failures: to protect, trust, hope, and persevere.

Love Bears All Things

Some of Jesus' opponents were trying to trap him, so they brought to him a woman caught in adultery. On any other day, they probably wouldn't have noticed her sin or cared about it, but on this day, she became a very humiliated pawn in their strategy against Jesus. These leaders rarely enforced the Old Testament punishment against people who committed adultery, and when they did, they did so very selectively and inconsistently. Still, God had condemned this kind of behavior long ago. So should this woman be stoned, as the law demanded? Or would Jesus publicly contradict the law by giving her a pass? Would he speak truth or grace?

At first, Jesus said nothing. He simply wrote in the dirt. Was he listing his opponents' sins? Listing other laws that they broke regularly? Writing some comment about the man involved? After all, if a woman was caught in adultery, so was a man—it takes two for things like this. Yet in their hypocrisy, no one brought her partner before Jesus. The Bible doesn't say what Jesus wrote, but the words he spoke were hard to argue with: "Let any one of you who is without sin be the first to throw a stone at her" (John 8:7). He stooped down to continue writing in the dirt again, and one by one, everyone left. With no accusers left, Jesus assured the woman that he didn't condemn her either. But he did tell her to go and sin no more.

Jesus covered this woman's sin. He took no pleasure in her humiliation; he refused even to participate in it. He became the defender of her value as a person without justifying what she had done. He didn't act like adultery wasn't an issue. Of course it's an issue. He acknowledged that it was sin and told her not to do it anymore. But that was the end of it. He wouldn't let her accusers

> Jesus protected her from her own failure.

condemn her or continue to humiliate her. He protected her from her own failure.

This is a beautiful picture of how love "protects," or, as some translations say, "bears all things." The word *stego* appears rarely in the New Testament—only four times and all in Paul's letters. It literally means "to cover," or even to endure or suffer. It conveys the sense of protecting something by covering it, even at some personal cost. In the context of failure, that would mean covering up someone's mistakes with silence, keeping a confidence, or hiding the errors and flaws of others.

Sometimes we feel empowered or superior by knowing "inside information" about someone else's fault, and there's a strong urge to pass that kind of information on to others—

just a little FYI or "did you know?" in an e-mail or phone conversation, sometimes even in the form of a prayer request. That's not loving. Love protects.

Some people "protect" by ignoring important issues or living in a state of denial, even when damaging behavior is destroying a relationship. That's not love either. Burying something that needs to be dealt with doesn't help anyone. And covering up an abusive situation can even be dangerous. So we clearly aren't talking about a passive, see-no-evil approach.

No, we all need someone to love us enough to see through our facade and deal with our faults, weaknesses, and sins. And we'll never make ourselves vulnerable enough for that kind of transparency unless we feel safe from humiliation and blame. We need people around us who will help us deal with our failures and grow from them, but without exposing and exploiting us in the process.

I tell you the following story with our son's permission. When my youngest son was a senior in high school, he came home from school one day and was greeted by his mother and me standing next to the computer in the back bedroom. Our ministry's IT department had cleaned up the computer I worked from home on and found a year's worth of pornography sites that had been visited.

My eyes met Ryan's, and after a quick denial, he blurted

out through tears about a yearlong struggle that started as a "pop-up" on our computer. We hugged, we prayed, we set boundaries, we wept, we walked through the pain together, and we watched God restore his mind and heart over the next couple of years.

Fast-forward a decade, Ryan and I were teaching on parenting and technology at the Billy Graham Training Center. Ryan helped parents learn what to do and not to do in helping their children. Then he said, "Create a safe environment where your kids know that no matter what they do, no matter how they may fail, that they truly can always come to you. It was the talks and times my dad and I had when I was little that let me know I could be completely honest later. That's where the healing happened." Although I made many mistakes as a parent, I am so grateful that Ryan and I started early in building trust and learning how to face our failures.

In other words, we need people to protect us from our own flaws. They can provide the truth and grace we need to grow, but then it's over. They keep it in confidence. They don't pass it on to anyone else. They don't make jokes about it. They don't even make an embarrassing, pseudo-spiritual prayer request out of it. It's covered.

There are a lot of people in the world who need to stop hearing about their failures. They are tired of being wounded by sarcastic comments, jokes, innuendo, and blame. A person who knows his or her guilt—and most people really are aware of their failures, even when they act like they aren't—starts to interpret every look or every ambiguous comment in the light of their failure. They get defensive and bitter. Only love can undo that.

Love takes the attitude Jesus demonstrated with the adulterous woman and every other fallen, broken person he met. It says, "I'm with you, let's deal with it." When we're living out this kind of love, the only reason we bring up a failure is to address it in a healthy, productive way, not to lay blame, rehash the past, or leverage guilt as motivation. We deal with it and move on. It just doesn't come up anymore. That's how love responds to people's failures. Who are the people in your world who need this kind of love? Are some of them in your family, your church, your office, and your neighborhood?

> Love says, "I'm with you, let's deal with it."

Love Believes All Things

One hot afternoon, Jesus and his disciples stopped in a town to rest. Most of the women of the town had come to get water from the well earlier in the day—that was the normal time for drawing the day's water—but one woman came in the afternoon. Apparently she wasn't "in" with the other women, maybe by her own choice or, more likely, by theirs.

The disciples had gone to look for food, and Jesus was alone at the well. He asked the woman for a drink. She was shocked that a Jewish man would ask for anything from a woman. Or a Samaritan. Or a . . . well, he couldn't have known that side of her. But if he knew who she was and what she had done, he surely wouldn't have anything to do with her.

But he started a conversation with her anyway and filled his words with both truth and grace. He looked into her life and saw her string of past relationships and her current immoral one. Apparently she had been looking for love in all the wrong places. He told her about the kind of water that truly satisfies a soul and the God who is looking for those who truly love him. He talked about a heavenly Father who pursues people who fail—even those who fail again and again. Even her.

This woman realized that the man at the well wasn't rejecting her, even though he knew about her immorality. He was calling her into something deeper, better, higher. In spite of everything he had discerned about her life, he believed in her.

That's what love does. It believes. In contrast to the

word for "protect," the word for "trust" or "believe" is used 239 times in the New Testament. It's the common word for "believe" or "commit" and is used in a lot of contexts, but in this case it means to have confidence in another person. Love trusts.

This isn't a naive trust. When someone has lied to us a hundred times, we don't "believe all things." That's just gullible. This kind of trust is discerning and insightful, but it still chooses to believe the best about someone. It avoids suspicion and judgment and doesn't assume the worst. When we hear a rumor or an accusation about someone, we choose to withhold judgment until we know the details. When someone's behavior seems to have negative consequences, we choose not to assume wrong motives. We believe or assume the best.

I had a great opportunity to practice this as I was studying this passage (1 Corinthians 13:6–8). A very important meeting was about to start, and we realized a key team member who was supposed to be there wasn't. I didn't know where he was, and neither did anyone else. And our minds can go to all kinds of places in that situation, can't they? It's easy to assume that the person just doesn't have his act together or doesn't care like the rest of us do or is just being a slacker. All of that passed through my mind, but so did this passage. I remember choosing to believe in him. I stopped the critical, judgmental thoughts dead in their tracks and deliberately thought, "Okay, I know the character of this team member. Maybe he had a flat tire. Maybe his wife is sick. Maybe one of the kids had an issue that had to be dealt with. Or maybe God showed him something that was more important and he's being obedient." And as it turns out, there was a good reason he was late. That may seem like a fairly trivial example, but these little incidents happen all the time and give us way too many opportunities to judge people unfairly. Love chooses not to assume the worst.

Instead, love decides to apply the best explanation for a situation, the one that puts the person in the most positive light. When someone seems to neglect her responsibility, love refuses to start wondering if maybe she's being irresponsible. When a spouse does the same annoying thing for the five hundredth time, love refuses to assume that things will never change. And when we give people the benefit of the doubt and they happen to fall short anyway, love applies enough grace to expect something better next

> Love decides to apply the best explanation for a situation, the one that puts the person in the most positive light.

time. It always thinks the best and tries to bring out the best in others.

Failure doesn't define a person. If it does, Scripture isn't true and our redemption isn't very effective. If God looked at us and defined our identity by what we've done wrong, we would have no hope. But God doesn't do that. He knows us by who we are becoming. He knows what he is shaping us into. He sees our future and is using every situation to conform us to the likeness of his Son. "He who began a good work in you will carry it on to completion until the day of Christ Jesus" (Philippians 1:6). That's his perspective.

So if that isn't our perspective on ourselves and others, we are disagreeing with God. Love compels us to respond to others' failures with the firm belief that failure doesn't define a person. Even though that person messed up, he or she is still God's child, still valued, still loved. Love says, "I believe in you."

I have a friend who's an extraordinarily gifted communicator and leader, but he seemed pretty discouraged recently. He was going through one of those times of getting hit with lots of spiritual darts, i.e., a negative e-mail one day, a critical comment the next, rumors and gossip that had him questioning his value and his role in God's kingdom. As I was praying one morning, I sensed God prompting me to go sit down and talk with him—to remind him how gifted he is and what God has been doing with his life. So I encouraged him not to believe the criticisms he had been getting lately and assured him that whatever he does in life, I'm behind him a hundred percent. Nothing major, no earth-shattering revelations, just some face-to-face encouragement. But his countenance started to change, just because somebody said, "I'm with you and I believe in you."

Who in your life needs to hear that? Who needs to know that dropping out of school, getting a divorce, getting fired, having an abortion, losing their life's savings, getting cut from the team, or any other failure or mistake doesn't define who they are or what they can become? People desperately need someone to still believe in them, even as we help them face their sin or failure. That kind of trust in the face of failure can change the course of a person's life.

Love Hopes All Things

Rahab spent much of her life as a prostitute, but that didn't prevent God from using her to help his people into the Promised Land. She secured her place in Israel's history and in the ancestry of the Messiah not because she had a spotless record but because she believed a promise and was willing to serve God.

Peter had completely abandoned Jesus, even cursed him and denied ever knowing him. I suspect that from God's point of view, that's a pretty big failure. Peter certainly felt that it was. But Jesus didn't define Peter by that failure. He knew Peter's future and, in the solid hope of that future, restored Peter to fellowship with him and a very fruitful ministry.

Saul was a sworn enemy of anyone who professed Jesus as Lord. And he didn't just oppose them with words; he tried, often successfully, to have them killed. But Jesus chose Saul, aka Paul, to carry his message throughout the Gentile world and to write much of the New Testament.

Those are just three examples of people who appeared to have no hope: a prostitute, a betrayer, and a murderer. Yet God not only forgave each one of them, he used them in magnificent ways. Why? Because failure doesn't define us. Because love not only protects and trusts, it also hopes.

> Failure doesn't define us. Love not only protects and trusts, it also hopes.

The kind of love that comes from God and flows through his people is filled with hope. The word *elpizo* implies a sense of expectation, a patient confidence. It's usually used in the context of salvation or deliverance—our hope in the forgiveness of sin, of deliverance from evil, and of Jesus' return and an eternal destiny in heaven. We anchor ourselves in the hope that no matter what's happening in our lives or how unfair it may be, we have a Savior. The God-man Jesus, who died and was raised from the dead, will rescue us and give us an eternal home with him. But in this passage this powerful word is used in the context of loving relationships. Real love is hopeful love.

Biblical hope is different from how we use the word today. We use it for wishful thinking. "I hope it doesn't rain." "I hope that investment pans out." "I hope this marriage works out better than his last three." That's a shot in the dark, a wish that things will go well without any definite expectation that they will. That's not what the Bible means when it speaks of hope.

Biblical hope is absolute confidence in the reality of what God has promised. It isn't about people having the power to change if they set their minds to it, or that circumstances will work out exactly the way we want them to. This hope is rooted in God's character, his promises, and his sovereignty. He is in absolute control, he will do what he has said, and he can redeem and completely transform any person or situation, no matter how hopeless that person or situation may appear.

Some people and circumstances in our lives look pretty

hopeless. Sometimes an addict goes through rehab after rehab and still hasn't made any significant change. Or a child lies again and again, and no matter what his parents try, he still lies. There are completely unsatisfying marriages in which one or both partners refuse to go to counseling and don't think they need to change. Or coworkers who make everyone around them crazy—and happen to be the ones in charge. You get to a point where you're completely out of emotional gas, where you've hoped again and again that some big breakthrough is going to happen and things are going to change, but you are repeatedly disappointed. After a while, you completely lose hope in your ability to fix the situation. You're at your wit's end.

But there's a hope that goes beyond our own resources, a hope that says, "I've done all I can do, and I'm not going to put my hope in this person anymore. I'm not going to trust that program to work or trust my ability to change things. I'm not going to wait for that 'aha' moment that will make everything wonderful. I'm going to trust that the all-knowing, all-powerful, sovereign, loving God knows about this situation and is going to work in it." We make a conscious decision to

> We make a conscious decision to believe that hopeless situations are never hopeless to God.

believe that hopeless situations are never hopeless to God. So even when we're at the end of our rope and ready to give up, even when failure seems to be final, there's always reason to hope in God's ability to redeem and restore. True love is rooted in that kind of hope.

I vividly remember a situation that occurred about twenty years ago in which I had completely lost hope. One of my sons and I were constantly butting heads, and I had no hope that any of my parenting would make a difference in his life. He was rebelling, and he had a young dad who was way too hard on him at the wrong times. It was a horrendous situation.

At one point, this son of mine told us Christianity just wasn't his thing. Theresa and I would sit up at night and talk and pray and cry, and I lost all hope that he would change, or that I had any parenting ability that would bring about change. But at a deeper level, I had hope that the God who changed Paul's life and raised Jesus from the dead could do something in his life. The journey was a hard and painful one. But God did a miracle!

About four years later, my son began leading worship. Then he had his own band. Eventually he began writing songs, and today some of his songs are being sung in worship services by millions of people around the world. I'm still amazed that someone I had no hope in and who represented my failures as a parent now writes songs about how great God is. That's why biblical hope is never out of place.

Love hopes all things because people like Peter can betray the Son of God himself and still become a leader of the early church and one of the most significant people in all of Christian history. Saul can be transformed from a terrorist who persecuted Christians to the faith's greatest spokesman and advocate. And you and the people around you can move from a place of absolute failure to great fruitfulness, even when it looks like all hope is lost. Love isn't based on how things look at the moment. Love chooses to hope.

Love Endures All Things

Joseph was sold into slavery by his brothers and later falsely accused of rape. His circumstances were the perfect recipe for bitterness. He spent years in servitude and prison because of the mistakes and evil intentions of others. But Joseph didn't buy in to the bitterness. He didn't let the pain of betrayal and lies cause him to give up and shut down. He stayed in God's program because he knew God was in control.

At the end of his life, after he had been made the second

most powerful person in Egypt and saved his own people, Joseph was able to tell his brothers that no one was holding their failures against them. "You intended to harm me, but God intended it for good," he explained. At the opportune moment, when he could have blasted them for their past sins, "he reassured them and spoke kindly to them" (Genesis 50:20–21).

That's the love that perseveres. We experience that love from God when we trust him. Nothing will enter our lives that he does not either decree or allow, and nothing will enter our lives that he cannot work out for our good. When a loved one is in the hospital, when a child is rebelling, when our debts are overwhelming—whatever crisis or trial we can go through—he is in control. That applies to the failures of others, even when those failures impact us severely. Because love *protects*, *trusts*, and *hopes*, it is also able to *persevere* in the face of its greatest challenges.

The word for "persevere" or "endure" is enlightening. *Hypomeno* comes from *hypo*—to be under—and *meno*—pressure, stress, misfortune, pain, difficulty. It has the sense of bravely and calmly bearing problems and ill treatment, of persevering under misfortune and trial. It also means "to remain." In

> Love sticks around, even when it has to put up with a lot.

other words, love stays. It sticks around, even when it has to put up with a lot.

That doesn't mean staying because of an inability to leave or to set appropriate boundaries. Codependent love says, "I have to stay in this abusive or dysfunctional relationship because I'm an incomplete person without it." Real love balances truth and grace, setting boundaries and dealing with things that shouldn't be tolerated. But it refuses to give up on somebody.

The opposite of this side of love is indifference. Many people think the opposite of love is hate, but at least there's still some passion in hate. The opposite of love that perseveres is simply deciding not to care anymore, to walk away saying, "Just forget it." Real love doesn't do that. It says, "I'm not giving up on you, no matter what." It remains engaged even when things are difficult. In spite of failures, even those that give you every right to leave, you choose to stick around because that is what God has done with each of us.

That's what Jesus did on the cross. He wasn't crucified by Romans or Jews, and it wasn't the nails that held him in place. Enduring love held him there because we had failed badly and would continue to do so. He took our sin on himself and gave himself as an offering for it. He experienced the wrath of God for our sins so we wouldn't have to. When our love perseveres—endures all things—we are demonstrating the kind of love Jesus showed us.

That's really the heart of the gospel. We don't become Christians or remain Christians by getting rid of our failure. We receive Jesus' perfection by faith. God loves us relentlessly, choosing to overcome our failures by giving us the life of Jesus. Instead of condemning us for our sin, he gives us a substitute. When we put our faith in Jesus, trusting what he has done for us, we are born into a new life. God's Spirit comes into us. We live not by trying to be good, read our Bibles, pray, give our money to the church, and do all the things we think are spiritual. We live by remaining in relationship with God and depending on his strength and love to live through us.

Not only is that a perfect illustration of the love described in 1 Corinthians 13, it's also the means by which we do less and love more. The Holy Spirit inside of us is not what drives us relentlessly toward a false finish line of success. He gives us a desire to be around the people we love, to invest our lives in others, and to enjoy the ways they invest

> Our life in Christ is primarily relational, not productive. It is love-oriented, not performance-oriented.

in us. Our life in Christ is primarily relational, not productive. It is love-oriented, not performance-oriented. It is to be immersed in and saturated with the love that Jesus demonstrated for us and that God now puts within us.

The Result: Love Never Fails

This kind of love never fails. The wording literally means that love never "falls down." It never gets corrupted or ruined. It never runs out of gas. When you love, situations and circumstances may not always come out the way you want them to, but you will never lose. That can't be said for your attempts to do more; you can accomplish a lot of work and still fail at life. But when you do less and love more, you can't lose. You can trust that even when things don't go your way, even when people fail you, even when circumstances seem to work against you, your life is governed by an all-wise, all-powerful God. We are free to invest in others and absorb their failures because God's love will never fail us.

This kind of love also applies to our own failures. God would not tell us to have the kind of love that perseveres and overcomes the failures of others if he wasn't willing to show that love to us when we fail. When we stop blaming our past, our parents, our culture, or those around us and simply admit that we have failed, he forgives. He stays. He loves with truth and grace, so when we are honest about not being a good follower of Jesus, not being a good spouse or parent or friend, not using words or money wisely, not being able to overcome an addiction, or any other shortcoming we have, he meets us in our failure and helps us get past it. That's truth and grace. That's love that bears all things, believes all things, hopes all things, and endures all things. And that's the kind of love that never fails.

∽◌ QUESTIONS FOR
Reflection/Discussion ◌∽

◌ How has God dealt with your failures? Do you believe he really deals with your failure in the way we're told to love others? Why or why not?

◌ Do you know someone whom God wants you to love in spite of the fact that he or she has failed you? If so, which of the following responses best fits the situation?

> ❧ covering the failure

> ❧ believing the best about them despite the circumstances

> ❧ trusting that God can and will work in them, even if the situation seems hopeless

> ❧ continuing to endure and helping them even when you don't have to

❧ Why is it important for your response to be both truthful and grace-filled?

❧ In any situation that came to mind as you read this chapter, what are your "next steps" of love? Ask those close to you to support you and help you implement those next steps, if needed.

SIX

In the Name of Love

"Pride (In the Name of Love)" is one of U2's most popular songs, but it's hard to figure out what the lyrics mean at first. The melody of the song came out in a jam session in Hawaii, and the lyrics were added later. In fact, lead singer Bono has lamented how some of the words really don't make sense—they are thrown together, sort of like shapes in an expressionist painting. The song is about Martin Luther King Jr., but that isn't apparent on the surface. Much of it just sounds like words that conveniently fit the melody and rhythm of the song.

So what does that song have to do with doing less and loving more? It hit me that we all do a lot of things "in the name of love" that don't make sense. We try hard and do some very good things with good intentions, but they don't always get the results we want. Sometimes we do things we call love that aren't loving at all. But it eases our conscience and justifies the decisions we make and the crazy schedules we keep.

Here's a little poem I wrote that gives a few examples of what we do "in the name of love."

We give and give and give some more,
yet still feel guilty for not giving "more."

We get up early and come home late,
leaving little time or energy to relate.

We seem to be always "on the go,"
but love requires the gear of "slow."

We start them early so they'll be a star,
then spend our weekends in the car.

We buy them computers and fancy phones,
only to discover they feel all alone.

We celebrate their role on the traveling team,
then wonder later why at church they're rarely seen.

We make success what we reward,
but show little passion for His Word.

We withhold honest feedback from a friend,
then watch them suffer the consequences yet again.

If you look carefully at the first line of each pair, you'll notice that each statement comes from a pretty good motive. Isn't it good to be generous? To work hard? To set your kids up for success? To protect a friend's feelings? Those desires aren't wrong in themselves. But sometimes our well-meaning efforts can produce some bad results. When the means become the end, or when our motives shift a little over time so that they aren't what they used to be, we can end up with consequences we don't really want.

So the question we want to ask in this chapter is this: Why does the pursuit of so many "good" things produce so many "bad" lives? We've noticed some of our same issues in the Corinthian church—a high-capacity, very gifted, cosmopolitan church that happens to show signs of immature, self-centeredness, conflict, and not knowing how

> Why does the pursuit of so many "good" things produce so many "bad" lives?

to love one another. On the surface, they are driven to live for God and do what's right, but they end up with a mess.

Apparently, the Corinthians' highest priorities in their fellowship were impressing one another and establishing a reputation for what they had and what they could do. They were suing each other, talking about each other, and trying to be more "spiritual" than each other. They were missing what really mattered.

We've looked closely at how real love responds to hurts, to differences, and to failure. Now we need to see how love responds to misplaced priorities. There's a difference between being motivated by love and knowing how to apply it. Most of us don't live the way we do because of indifference. We love our families and friends. The problem is that our love is misapplied.

It's easy to see the difference between motives and application in extreme examples. You can have great motives when you bail someone out of financial or legal trouble, but your love is out of line if you never deal with their root issues and behaviors that get them into trouble. People think they're being sympathetic when they help an addict get by "this one time" or help them avoid the consequences of their behavior, but that's really enabling, prolonging, and deepening the addiction. That's not the kind of "covering" love does. So it's very possible to have motives that appear loving but produce results that are very harmful and unloving. "Loving more" doesn't only mean "doing less"; if it's real, authentic love, it also means doing some things differently.

I'm sure the Corinthians wanted to do the right thing. Most of them weren't willfully disobeying God. In fact, they were trying to fulfill his purposes for them. But they all seemed to have a different idea about how to do that. Just as we do some unwise things in the name of love, so did they. They had their priorities out of line.

Question #4: How Does Love Respond to Misplaced Priorities?

Love never fails. But where there are prophecies, they will cease; where there are tongues, they will be stilled; where there is knowledge, it will pass away. For we know in part and we prophesy in part, but when perfection comes, the imperfect disappears. When I was a child, I talked like a child, I thought like a child, I reasoned like a child. When I became a man, I put childish ways behind me. Now we see but a poor reflection as in a mirror; then we shall see face to face. Now I know in part; then I shall know fully, even as I am fully known. And now these three remain: faith, hope and love. But the greatest of these is love. (1 Corinthians 13:8–13)

We've noted that this beautiful chapter on love is actually a correction of misplaced priorities in the church. Paul makes a sweeping, absolute statement that love never fails. But almost everything else—even good spiritual gifts and practices—is temporary. In fact, a lot of what the church has been doing is childish, and Paul tells the Corinthians to grow up. There's a difference between what lasts and what doesn't, and the key to real love is focusing on what lasts.

This is where the rubber meets the road if we really want to simplify our lives. If, a few months or a few years down the road, we want to find ourselves in better, more meaningful relationships and with much less stress than we have now, we need to take this truth to heart: love ruthlessly refuses to allow temporal "good" things to crowd out the eternal "best" things.

> Love ruthlessly refuses to allow temporal "good" things to crowd out the eternal "best" things.

In other words: love cannot and will not place the good above the best.

Why does love have to be "ruthless" in the choices it makes? Because some people may not like your new priorities. Because loving with proper priorities may mean less affirmation in some areas where you're used to being affirmed. There are lots of reasons this won't be comfortable at first, and plenty of temptations to circumvent or abandon the process. But minor adjustments have a tendency to become really minor or even nonexistent after a few days. You end up just as overscheduled or overwhelmed as before. Change has to be decisive and significant. And you have to be ruthless for it to last.

It won't help to tweak your schedule or get a little bit more margin to do a few more important things. You'll need to take some pretty radical steps to get there. It may mean changing whole sections of your life. Refocusing sometimes comes at the expense of what seems to matter now. But if you're serious about getting past some of those relational issues, living more simply, and building more meaning into your life, you can do it by putting ruthless love into practice.

So how does love respond to misplaced priorities? It recognizes the difference between what is temporary and what is lasting, and it chooses the long-term view. The gifts of the Spirit won't last forever. They aren't needed in heaven. Faith, hope, and love never go out of style. They last for all eternity. And love is the greatest of the three.

THESIS: Love Is Supreme—Our Number One Priority

Paul's thesis is that love is supreme. It's the number one priority. No matter what else is on our agenda, love trumps all of it. Why? Because love never fails. It will never be corrupted. It's permanent.

> No matter what else is on our agenda, love trumps all of it.

Love is the characteristic that best describes God (1 John 4:8, 16). That's what sets his agenda. Love governs all his other attributes. This is how he interacts with us. So it only makes sense that if we are being transformed to be like him, love is going to have to become the number one priority in our lives too.

Is love what people would see if they picked up your schedule or your checkbook? If someone could read your thoughts during your mental downtime, when your mind wanders wherever it wants to go, would they see a story of someone who really loves God and really loves people? At a practical level in your relationship with God, do your greatest desires line up with his greatest commandments—to love him and to love others?

Many of us would have to say no. Sure, most people—even many non-Christians—would say that love is the most important thing in the world. Those who believe in the Bible would agree that our purpose in life is to fulfill the greatest commandment of loving God and loving others. But when we look at our time, money, dreams, and directions, are we really lining up with our ideals? We have to wonder if we're fooling ourselves.

CONTRAST: The Best of Temporal Things Are Far Less Important Than Love

It's especially easy to fool ourselves when we mistake spiritual service and gifts for love. That drive for significance and meaning sometimes plays out in church. Instead of achieving more in business, for example, we invest ourselves in serving the body of Christ with whatever gifts he has given us. That's important to do, of course; we're supposed to serve one another with the spiritual gifts we've been given. But are we driven to do that because we're "looking for love," as we talked about in the last chapter? Or are we serving as an expression of our love? It's not always easy to tell the difference. If we find ourselves overly concerned with our image, our reputation, or our recognition when we serve, there's a pretty good chance we've just added the church to our false attempts to find acceptance and approval. We can get wrapped up in the activity and still miss the priority.

Paul says that even powerful, beneficial spiritual gifts are less important than love. Love has to be the motive behind everything. The gifts are given for the extremely important task of growing God's kingdom, but they still aren't most important. Prophecies will cease. Speaking in tongues will go away. Even our partial knowledge—or at least the means by which we currently get spiritual understanding—will pass away. None of them will be needed when Jesus comes back and we see him face-to-face. But love? It's forever.

Think about how this might apply to our churches and families. It's important to give our time and resources to the ministries and people around us, but if all we do is give without ever getting refreshed, it simply leads to guilt and burnout. It's good to give our children experiences that

Do you see how good things can lead to bad results? That always happens when love isn't the highest priority in our lives.

will help them grow, but if that means spending every weekend in a minivan without any time for a heart connection, it simply leads to a lot of activity and not much relationship. It's good to be a faithful employee who goes the extra mile, but if that means getting up at five-thirty every morning and coming home at eight every night, it simply leads to lots of achievement and not much personal growth or time with God and others. Do you see how good things can lead to bad results? That always happens when love isn't the highest priority in our lives.

THE REASON: *They Don't Last*

The reason great ministry activities—Paul lists prophecy, tongues, and spiritual knowledge as examples—still don't measure up to love is that they don't last. The things we do by faith are great, but they won't be needed forever. "Perfection" is coming—there will be a completion and a fulfillment of all things when Jesus comes back. There won't be any need for most of our ministry activities. We're going to know him fully just as we've been already fully known.

Paul is saying, "Look, you're so into arguing about this gift or that one and who's really spiritual and who is not that you fail to recognize what all these gifts have in common: they're temporal." It isn't that they don't matter. They just don't matter *most*.

There's a lot of pressure in our society to redefine what really matters, and it's all very tempting to buy in to it. We're told that you're not a good dad if you don't spend every weekend helping your kids hit the ball right or getting them to all their practices. Or that you won't make it as a single person unless you hang out with a "certain" group, wear designer clothes, and be up on the latest culture. Or that you aren't successful if you don't drive a certain car or own a nice enough house. And so we spin our wheels trying to live up to these artificial standards and usually end up feeling pretty guilty for not measuring up or burned out for trying so hard to "make it."

But "make" what? A false standard of success? Do we really want to make it big and go through two or three marriages on the way? Or be successful professionally and have kids who don't know us and don't really want to?

There are pitfalls in every area of life, including ministry. I have a pastor friend in another country who has a very fruitful ministry that impacts tens of thousands of people. He teaches in a seminary, runs the administrative side of a very large church, and speaks at conferences. But his family life is suffering. His little girl doesn't see him very often, as he's up by 4 A.M. and home after 8 P.M. He is working the equivalent of almost three full-time jobs and holds advanced degrees from elite schools in his country and the United States. His honest confession is, "I feel trapped." He is involved in good spiritual activities, but gets undesirable results. Why? Misplaced priorities.

We all do a lot of things "in the name of love" that don't

produce love's fruit. It isn't that the good things we do don't matter. They matter a lot. They just aren't the highest priority. We've put them in a higher place than they belong. In order to love more—authentically and deeply—we have to rearrange our priorities and do fewer of the activities that enslave us.

> We do a lot of things "in the name of love" that don't produce love's fruit.

A lot of people realize this when they get to the end of their lives, and then it's too late. They look back with regret. They wonder what would have happened if they had blocked off time with God for a half hour every day, or if they had eaten together as a family several nights a week, or if instead of watching TV every evening, they invested more in the people who really matter to them. We need to have that end-of-life perspective now while we can still turn our hearts toward the things that matter most and that last forever.

Twenty years ago, I heard a pastor use an illustration that helped me capture this truth.[4] Imagine throwing a big party for a special celebration and commissioning an elaborate ice sculpture to be the centerpiece of the decorations. The ice artists get an enormous block of ice, come up with a beautiful design, and begin to sculpt it with their chain saws and chisels. After weeks of work, the time for the celebration comes. The sculptors roll out their twenty-foot-high ice masterpiece, complete with multicolored lights slowly rotating in the center of the outdoor gala affair. Thousands of people "ooh" and "aah" over how amazing it is. It's truly impressive. The sculpture becomes the talk of the party.

Several hours later, as volunteers are cleaning up after the party, the ice sculpture is mostly a big puddle of water. It was beautiful while it lasted, but there's hardly anything left. The artists' work was excellent and admired by all, but it didn't last.

I wonder how many of us are laboring with excellence, giving our best energy and time to some "very good things" that simply won't last. I wonder how much of that is rooted in our desire for temporal applause and the pressure to impress. I wonder if these sincere but misplaced priorities might be what keeps our lives so complicated and our relationships so shallow. What do you think? What demands and pressures are you living with that will melt

> I wonder how many of us are laboring with excellence, giving our best energy and time to some "very good things" that simply won't last.

when it's all said and done? And how do we break out of this addiction to the temporal?

THE SOLUTION: Grow Up

So how exactly do we do this? Paul's answer is simple: grow up. That's how love responds to misplaced priorities. When we're children, we talk like children, think like children, and reason like children. But when we grow up, we put away childish things. We talk, think, and reason like adults.

These three verbs—*talk*, *think*, and *reason* in verse 11—are very revealing. They show us a lot about the difference between children and adults.

Think about how kids interact. What do they talk about? It's all about what they want. That's their focus. It doesn't matter if there are fifty toys on the floor, two toddlers will find one to argue over and say, "I want it!" They are always asking for something to have or something to do.

What do children think about? Usually themselves. They are very me-focused. I've never heard a child walk into a roomful of other children and ask, "Everyone doing okay? What's really going on in your life? Need any juice or milk? Got enough to play with?" I've never seen a young child wake up in the morning thinking about how to encourage mom or dad today. They don't sit down with the other kids just to check in and see how they are doing. No, young children are very focused on their own needs and wants and interests.

They are also focused on the "right now." That's how they reason. If you offer a child one candy bar now or two if they wait a few days, most will go for the one now. A few days from now is too far into the future to think about. They see their needs and wants as immediate.

This is the picture Paul paints of the Corinthian Christians and their misplaced priorities. They were interested in their wants, focused on themselves, and using short-term reasoning. Paul was basically calling them childish.

But there's a more excellent way. When we become adults, we put away childish attitudes—at least in theory. That isn't to say that all adults are mature, of course. That's why Paul had to remind the Corinthians what adults act like. But we recognize someone as mature when he or she begins to leave childish ways behind and adopts adult attitudes.

So what's different about adults? When we mature, we talk less about what we want and more about what's needed in any given situation. What's the best for everyone involved? What's the right solution? That's how an adult ought to talk.

When we become adults, we begin to realize that life isn't all about us. Our thinking gravitates toward others. We develop an outward focus. Mothers, for example, don't wake up in the morning thinking about how to spend the day on themselves. That isn't an option. The kids aren't going to feed and bathe themselves. Responsibility calls. We have to think about the needs of others.

> When we become adults, we begin to realize that life isn't all about us.

And when we mature, we learn to look down the road and plan ahead. We take the long-term view. We forsake immediate gratification because the benefits of delayed gratification are so much better. So our questions shift from "What can I have now?" to "What is best for the greatest amount of people in the long run?" That's an adult perspective.

The Corinthians didn't have that and, frankly, neither do many of us. We may think we're looking way down the road and planning wisely for the benefit of others, but we're fooling ourselves if we think sacrificing relational depth for more money, more education, more experiences, and more opportunities for more of the same is worth the cost. In the long run, relational depth matters. Love is the highest priority.

THE PRINCIPLE: Cloudy Vision
Leads to Complexity, but Clear Vision Leads to Love

Mirrors in the ancient world weren't very clear, not like they are today. An ancient mirror was polished bronze or brushed steel, and it rendered a pretty cloudy image. You could tell the face looking into it was yours, but it wasn't a precise picture. It was still hard to see.

That's what our vision is like right now, Paul says. We don't see everything clearly. A time is coming when we will. When Jesus returns, we will see fully and, according to 1 John 3:2, we will be like him. Completely transformed.

It's our cloudy vision that leads to the complexity in our lives. We hear demands coming from several directions, and we feel pulled. There are demands for family and for work and for church and for our own dreams and goals. Most of us struggle to figure out which ones to choose, so we try to do them all. But we end up not doing any of them well, and we neglect our own souls.

> Most of us struggle to figure out which ones to choose, so we try to do them all.

When things get clear, we don't feel pulled in every direction like we do now. When we have a clear vision of where we're going, of what really matters most, we won't get tossed around by pressures and demands that don't serve our best interests.

When we learned that Theresa had cancer, I experienced a clarity of vision like never before. I confess, I am one of those people who struggles with "what's really best," and as a result, I try to do too much. Overextension has been a lifelong battle for me. But on December 6, 2010, the day we got the news, it became very clear what mattered most. Within a week, I canceled all speaking and all travel for the next six months. It was easy! No second thoughts, no sense that I might miss an opportunity or the ministry might miss a beat. Why? When you love more, you do less. We went through the surgery and then months of treatments together. I somehow had time to drive her to every appointment.

Knowing I might not have much time with the person I love the most completely transformed my priorities. Interestingly enough, I had multiple people at church sense my preaching had a new power, and to our amazement, Living on the Edge's ministry grew in my absence.

When you really get clear, you won't buy things you don't need with money you don't have in order to impress people who don't care. You won't immerse yourself in entertainment that essentially feeds you the philosophies of the world—childish perspectives that focus on here and now and me-me-me. You won't worship your work or climb upward on a ladder you aren't even sure you want to be on. Seeing clearly reduces complexity and produces spiritual simplicity.

That's the heart of what we've been dealing with in this chapter. A wrong value system complicates our lives and ultimately results in emptiness. That's why we have to put away childish ways and grow up. Our natural vision isn't enough; we have to know that when we see Jesus face-to-face, our new clarity of vision will reveal faith, hope, and love as precious treasures, with love being supreme among them. Why is love the greatest? It lasts! Forever! Faith is believing in what we can't see—the promises and character of God—but someday faith becomes sight. Hope anchors our souls in the certainty of God's plan, but at some point the plan is fulfilled. We will one day possess what we once hoped for. But love continues on. It never fails. When we meet Jesus face-to-face, love will take center stage. Are you beginning to see why love is the secret to simplifying your life? It's not about trying harder to "do less." It's about seeing clearer to love more.

If you're coming to grips with some misplaced priorities right now, don't be too hard on yourself. You live in a complex world that can be very competitive. It's dog eat dog, survival of the fittest, or even just survival period. There are pressures and demands from every direction, many of them competing against each other. Some of them have very valid rationales. It's understandable when we get confused about which priorities are highest. So this isn't a matter of God getting

> If you're coming to grips with some misplaced priorities right now, don't be too hard on yourself.

mad at us for misplaced priorities; it's our heavenly Father telling us there's something better than getting several years down the road and realizing all our efforts have turned into puddles of water. He has plenty of grace for us and understands how we got where we are. There's a reason we see in a mirror dimly. We've been handed a dim mirror.

But we've also been handed a glimpse of heaven's perspective, and it gives us a much better standard to go by. When we start asking adult questions like "What's really important?" and "What's wisest in the long run?" it gives us some pretty clear answers. So if we see in part but want to uncloud our vision, we can turn to the revelation that promises to guide our feet and light our path. We have to get into God's Word. That's not a legalistic instruction to read your Bible; that's just the primary communication in this love relationship with our heavenly Father. When we're confused, we can ask him a question and wait for his direction. He has a way of getting his truth into us when we're open to it, usually by opening up something in his Word that hits our hearts at the right time in the right way. For people who see dimly, that's indispensable.

That will help us when we ask the hard questions about whether both parents need to have a job, or whether a few extra hours of work each night is a wise investment of time, or whether the kids need to have cell phones at this age, or any of the other questions we wrestle with. The specific answers for each question aren't in the Bible, but the guiding principles are, and God's voice is available to us when we ask him for guidance. Regardless of what we decide on such issues, we know it's nonnegotiable for every member of our family to make time to love God, to connect deeply with one another, and to extend this love to those around us.

That's really the point of living more simply. It's not to develop a weird, alternative religious lifestyle. It's to be set apart as God's, to experience him and the very best he has to offer us. It means that people around us see in us a refreshing, deep, peaceful connection with God that flows out of our time with him and with others. It means providing a clear contrast to the relentless race with no finish line.

If we make loving God and others our highest priority, we may encounter some resistance or some discomfort in the transition. But God is big enough to take care of anything we have to overcome. He designed us for a life of peace that finds its pleasure and fulfillment in him.

~ QUESTIONS FOR
Reflection/Discussion ~

- How can our seemingly best motives actually be unloving in their long-term impact?

- In what ways have some good activities kept you from the best investment of your life and energy?

- How do you need to grow up in your talking, thinking, and reasoning in order to address misplaced priorities? What might this look like practically?

- What's your next step of faith and/or obedience in order to realign your priorities around what matters most and will last forever?

SEVEN

What the World Needs Now

$\mathcal{M}$y daughter Annie and I were taking a road trip recently, and the rental car we were driving had satellite radio. We were having a hard time staying awake, so she said, "Why don't we see what's on?"

There's no shortage of stations on satellite radio, so we would find a song we knew and sing along for a while, then change to another station. We went through about fifty stations in a couple of hours just to stay awake. And most of these stations were playing songs about love—finding it, losing it, wanting it, getting it, wanting it some more, and on and on. We heard country love, hip-hop love, alternative love, easy-listening love . . . love, love, love.

It's pretty obvious that love is what the world wants. In

fact, it reminded me of another popular old song from the sixties: "What the World Needs Now" by Hal David and Burt Bacharach. It's a sentimental little song, but it's absolutely true. We were designed for love. That's exactly what the world needs.

Our cell phones and computers have little receivers in them that are constantly looking for a connection. Sometimes they display a small graphic that spins around to show that they are searching for a signal. When they find one, they can send and receive information. But as soon as you change locations, they start searching again. They are always trying to connect.

Just like a cell phone, each of us has a receiver built into us that is constantly searching for love. From the moment we are born, something inside of us is reaching up and out to get connected—to be affirmed, to be cared for, to be held, to be valued. If we don't have that, we keep spinning until we find it somewhere. We crave that connection, not based on what we accomplish or how we look, but simply for who we are. That need for love will last until we take our last breath. It never goes away.

> From the moment we are born, something inside of us is reaching up and out to get connected.

There's only one place to find the kind of love we need, but unlimited ways we look for it. We talked about many of those ways in chapter 4. If we find love in the right place and the right way, it simplifies life. If we don't, bad stuff happens and life gets a lot more complicated. When we are not deeply and personally loved in ways that make sense to us, we will settle for any number of pseudo-love substitutes.

One of those substitutes is the *affirmation* we receive from success. People tell us, "You're good at that!" "Wow, you scored a lot of points." "You're smart." We love affirmation, and we usually go in whatever directions we're affirmed in. In other words, we do whatever gets us the most strokes. When someone tells us that we did a great job, that we're really gifted in a certain area, that we're smart or funny or creative, it feels a lot like love. Affirmation is good, but it isn't love. It's a substitute.

Another substitute is the *adulation* we receive from fame. Everyone wants their fifteen minutes, or even to rub shoulders with or drop names of people who have had their fifteen minutes. If you're a celebrity, even for a moment, you're suddenly important. Somehow we equate the two. The adulation looks a lot like love, but it isn't. It's people falling in love with an image. It's not the real thing.

Neither is the temporary sense of *intimacy* we get from illicit sex. Loneliness and pain drive our love receptor in search of a connection, and many people try to get that connection with online images or in an affair—anything to fill the hole. The illusion of intimacy is powerful, but it's temporary and shallow. It feels good, but it can leave emotional scars, diseases, and unwanted pregnancies—consequences that can last a lifetime.

The *attention* we receive for our possessions and image can look like love too. Our desire for attention drives multibillion-dollar image businesses like cosmetics and fitness and fashion. When we get attention for how we appear, it looks a lot like love. There's nothing wrong with looking good and feeling good, but the attention that comes from it is a poor substitute. It's based on an image, not on the real you.

So is the *esteem* that comes from position. We want to be a "somebody," and we can be if we get the corner office, make the team, have the right letters after our name, or have a club membership. We feel like somebody by having the position, and we think we're loved because of the esteem the position brings. Esteem can be nice, but it isn't love.

The *security* we perceive in wealth is an illusion as well. We get up early and go to bed late in order to earn enough to provide a sense of provision—security and safety that protects against unexpected expenses, a sour economy, or a job loss. Security feels like love, but it isn't. And our attempts to arrange for it make our lives more and more complex.

---

affirmation from success ≠ love

adulation from fame ≠ love

intimacy from illicit sex ≠ love

attention from possessions or image ≠ love

esteem from position ≠ love

security from wealth ≠ love

All of these substitutes are based on what we do or the image we present, not on who we actually are. Our quest to be loved deeply and personally creates fast-paced, overextended, complex lives driven to obtain success, fame, sex, looks, position, power, and wealth in the desperate hope that someday, someway, we will be loved . . . just for who we are!

Do you see the irony in that? Our little search engine that's always looking for a connection to real love can be tricked into thinking it has that connection when it finds substitutes for love. So we end up getting "love" for who we aren't rather than what we really crave—love for who we are.

As a result, we start to find our identity in our image, activities, and occupations; and we link our identity with the love we think we're receiving. So not only are we complicating our lives in this quest for love, we're complicating them in a way that ties our very identity to the complications. When we begin to stop our fast-paced, overextended lifestyle, it feels like we're letting go of ourselves. No wonder it's hard to break away.

But what we do is not the same as who we are. We aren't going to find real love in things like our position or possessions or appearance. Our lives get incredibly complex because our drive to find love leads us to success, fame, sex, looks, position, power, and wealth. We forget that it really is possible to have the love we need simply by being ourselves.

> Our lives get incredibly complex because our drive to find love leads us to success, fame, sex, looks, position, power, and wealth.

So if love is what the world needs, that raises three questions:

- Where do you find it?

- How do you get it?

- How do you give it away?

Where Do You Find Love?

The apostle John tells us exactly where to find love:

> *Dear friends, let us love one another, for love comes from God. Everyone who loves has been born of God and knows God. Whoever does not love does not know God, because God is love. . . . This is how we know that we live in him and he in us: He has given us of his Spirit.* (1 John 4:7–8, 13)

The kind of love that's unconditional, that's focused on who we are and not what we accomplish, comes first and foremost from God himself. He's the source. According to the passage above, the love you need is in your soul; the only thing that will ever fill you up is the love of God.

And John says that when you know God, when you are loved by him, one of the evidences will be that you will naturally overflow in love relationships to others. Not only does that cultivate fulfilling relationships, it also makes you one of the most attractive people in the world. Why? Because that's who people want to be around. No one wants to be around people consumed with themselves. When you're known for being a loving person, others are drawn to you.

We all want to be loving people, but it isn't always easy. And most of us know God loves us, at least theoretically. But there's a difference between knowing about God's love and actually experiencing it at a deep, heartfelt level. If God is the source, then knowing his love is the key to becoming loving ourselves. But what does that look like? What does it mean to be loved by God?

It isn't enough just to read what the Bible says about God's love. We actually have to believe it—to think about it, let it saturate our lives, and let it really sink in. John says that love comes from God, that everyone who loves God is born of him and knows him. Why? Because God is love.

If this is God's primary attribute, if this is the one characteristic that governs his relationship with us, then it needs to fully occupy our minds whenever we think about him. Each of us needs to know we are the object of his affection. Before we focus on doing the right things, being holy, finding our calling, praying, disciplining ourselves to read the Bible, or anything else we consider vital to following Jesus, we need to live in his love. Thoroughly.

Zephaniah 3:17 is a powerful picture that has helped me grasp God's love. It begins with "The Lord your God is with you. . . ."

The Lord your God is with you,
He is mighty to save.
He will take great delight in you;
He will quiet you with his love,
He will rejoice over you with singing.
(Zephaniah 3:17 NIV)

Part of being loved is knowing you won't be abandoned. That's what "Immanuel" means in Isaiah's prophecy of Jesus. He is "God with us." In our hardest trials and deepest needs, he is there.

> Part of being loved is knowing you won't be abandoned.

But he isn't just there; he is "the Mighty Warrior who saves." We usually interpret that word *saves* in terms of forgiveness of sins—our eternal salvation. And while that's true, the biblical word has a much more comprehensive meaning. It's about being delivered from trouble. Whenever we get in a jam, whenever we're mired in some problem, God is able to step in and save the day. He powerfully delivers us.

The verse goes on to say that God delights in us. A lot of people see his love as an obligation. He loves us because he has to, sort of like a parent loves a problem child in spite of his problems. But God doesn't just love us out of obligation. He delights in us. He actually *likes* us. He enjoys the love that he has for us. It gives him great pleasure.

Notice that his delight is "in you." That means it isn't based on what you do. It has nothing to do with your position or accomplishments. In fact, Zephaniah's prophecy was written to people who had blown it. It's a prophecy of restoration, not because people had done the right things but because God loved them. After God had created billions of galaxies, filled them with innumerable stars and planets, and displayed his artistry throughout the universe, he made human beings as the pinnacle of his creation. You and I are made in his image, designed specifically for a relationship with him. He wants to spend time with you, talk with you, and bless you. He enjoys you and wants to bring out the best in you.

The prophet says that after God restores his people, he will quiet them with his love. That's good news for people who are stressed out. I hear from people all the time who are overwhelmed by their complicated lives, and their plea is that they just want some peace. We want peace in our work schedules, peace in our marriages, peace in all the issues and concerns that keep us up at night. We want to unload all our issues and concerns and have that sense of freedom that says, "No matter what's going on, it will be okay." God promises to quiet us with his love—to bring some calm back into the relationship when our anxieties rise up. He wants to tell us, "I know you're going through a hard time right now, I know about your struggles, I know you've waited a long time for things to happen, but I want you to know I've got it all taken care of. It's going to be okay. No matter what happens, I love you, I'm with you, I'll protect you." That quiets us down.

For many of us, that happens through a human relationship. There are times when I'm completely overwhelmed and write down all the things I'm struggling with. And I'll sit with Theresa and say, "Honey, I know I'm not supposed to be anxious, but I'm feeling really stressed out. I've laid all this out before God in my journal, but I just need to talk through some things." And I know that no matter what happens, she's going to love me tomorrow the same way she loves me today. That "quieting down" that we experience in secure human relationships is the kind of quieting God wants to do for us. He has unlimited resources, we're the object of his affection, and he wants to quiet our hearts with his love.

Finally, God rejoices over us with singing. The picture is

of God holding us like a helpless baby. I've watched Theresa do this when our kids were small, and again now that we have grandkids. I can hear her in the next room holding the little ones and singing over them to calm their crying. Like a proud parent, God tenderly takes each of us in his arms and sings quietly to calm us down. His love and delight come through in the way he holds us. He rejoices over us, full of pride in his children. He feels deeply for every one of us. And this includes you—today, right where you are!

How would that impact your life if it really stuck in your heart? Can you imagine how free you would feel and how many issues you could push off to the side if you really felt God's love deep down inside? Your search for affirmation, attention, intimacy, esteem, and every other expression of love you seek would take a different—and much simpler—direction. This is why Paul prayed that the Ephesians would be strengthened within them to know the height and depth and length and breadth of God's incomprehensible love. We won't ever grasp it fully, but we can experience it. And life gets a whole lot simpler when we do.

How Do You Experience This Love?

God Deposits His Love in His Followers' Hearts Through His Spirit

> *We know that we live in him and he in us, because he has given us of his Spirit. And we have seen and testify that the Father has sent his Son to be the Savior of the world. If anyone acknowledges that Jesus is the Son of God, God lives in him and he in God. And so we know and rely on the love God has for us.* (1 John 4:13–16)

So how can we actually make that connection with God's love so that our hearts are getting what they were designed for? We know the fact that he loves us. How do we make it real in our experience?

The passage above from 1 John says that we live in him and he in us because he has given us his Spirit. That's our connection. If anyone acknowledges or "confesses" that Jesus is the Son of God—i.e., if anyone agrees with that truth—God lives in him, and he lives in God.

So there's a condition to experiencing and receiving God's love. Jesus, fully God and fully man, died on the cross to pay for our sins. He's our sin substitute. If we confess and acknowledge that, we enter into that connection with him. It isn't about our good works or how religious we are. If we turn from our sin, receive God's forgiveness through Christ's death as our substitute, the Spirit of God comes into our mortal body and takes up residence there. He will then manifest the power and presence of the living God.

When We Are Filled with the Holy Spirit, the Overflow Is Love

That's how our receiver connects. Through that connection, God wants to download adoption and forgiveness and place us in his family. He seals us with his Spirit, gives us spiritual gifts, and fills us with the same power that raised Jesus from the dead. And when we're filled with and controlled by his Spirit, the outcome is love. That's the overflow of his life inside of us. Galatians 5:22–23 describes the fruit of the Spirit as love, joy, peace, patience, kindness, goodness, faithfulness, gentleness, and self-control. All of this—his presence, his power, and being the object of his affection—is available to us.

We can miss it, though. *One way* we miss the experience of these things is to live outside of Christ—i.e., never accepting him into our lives. I spent the first eighteen years of my life intellectually aware of God's love, but I had never turned from my life of sin and self-will and asked Christ to forgive me and come into my life. Once I did that, I was born spiritually. That's when we experience forgiveness and that's when his Spirit comes into our lives and we are justified. We're declared righteous before God because of what Christ did for us. We can't know God's love for ourselves unless we've asked Christ to forgive us and come into our lives.

The *second way* we miss God's love is similar to what I experience on my iPad. Sometimes I'm working on it, and all of a sudden I can't send e-mail or receive it. I can't connect to a network. I've got the device, I've paid my bill, I've been connected, but now it isn't working. Why? There's interference. The signal gets dropped.

We're like that. We can have the Spirit living inside of us, fully connecting us with God, but if there's interference—if he isn't in control, if we're saying no to him, nurturing sin in our lives and not nurturing the connection we have with him—he withholds our experience of his love. He doesn't withhold his love; nothing changes that. But we lose our awareness and enjoyment of it. If we confess our sins, however, he is faithful to forgive us, cleanse us, and restore the connection (see John 1:9).

How Do You Get This Love?

I remember reading years ago about a "boy in a bubble"—a boy whose lack of an immune system required him to live in a completely sterile environment. His parents had to pass things in to him through the plastic wall of the bubble. They loved him and longed to hold him, but they could never contact him directly. He never experienced a personal touch.

A lot of Christians live like that. It's possible to agree with all we've talked about regarding having a personal relationship with God and being filled with his Spirit, and to still feel lonely or depressed. We know about God's love and have his Spirit living inside of us. We've given our lives to him and can agree with the conditions we've already discussed above. We know God longs to connect with us, encourage us, and hold us. We know he cares. But there's still a bubble. We still feel lonely and discouraged. We don't feel his personal touch.

So you may be reading this and thinking, "Yeah, I desperately need to connect with God's love. I really want that. But my life is crazy, and I'm just not experiencing it." Part of how you experience that is by stopping and talking to him. This is where doing less clearly opens up the door to loving—and being loved—more. He wants to give us grace and speak to us, but for some of us, it's been a while since we made time to listen. If you'll simplify your life, quit chasing the wind, and be quiet before him, he'll show up. One way or another, he will connect with us because we were designed to be loved by him.

> If you'll simplify your life, quit chasing the wind, and be quiet before him, he'll show up.

Knowing God's love and experiencing it are two different things, so let's make this really practical. As much as his Word reassures us about his love, and as much as his Spirit is present with us, it's really only in the context of daily life and its challenges that we experience his love in a hands-on way. God has designed at least *three ways* for his love to be worked into our lives at a practical level.

1. God Designed Love to Be Expressed in Our Spiritual Family

One of the ways God helps us experience love is through the physical bodies of others around us. Through their words and arms and kindness, we get to experience his love. He puts us in a spiritual family when his Spirit comes into us; we're all related to everyone else who is born of his Spirit. So ideally, Christians express God's love to one another and become the physical manifestation of that spiritual reality.

So when we have a deep need and other believers step up to meet that need, we aren't just experiencing their generosity; we're experiencing God's tangible touch through them. When we're in pain and another Christian comes alongside us to encourage and comfort, we aren't just benefiting from their compassion; we're encountering God's compassion through them. We are commanded to meet each other's needs, bear each other's burdens, speak words of encouragement and kindness to each other, and build each other up. You may have Christian relationships that fall short of this, but that's the ideal. And if you keep looking for that kind of relationship and invest yourself in those people, you'll experience God's love through them.

Paul wrote about this in his second letter to the Corinthians. God "comforts us in all our troubles, so that we can comfort those in any trouble with the comfort we ourselves receive from God" (2 Corinthians 1:4). The picture is of God's people receiving his love not only for their immediate needs but also to pass it on to others later when they have a need. This is why people who have been through a divorce are so well equipped to minister to those going through a divorce now, or why people who have overcome anxieties or addictions or abuse are able to speak God's truth and love into people struggling with those particular problems. Each of us is designed to be a conduit of grace through whom God shows himself. As we walk with our fellow believers, we come to know his love more deeply.

> Each of us is designed to be a conduit of grace through whom God shows himself.

2. God Designed Love to Be Birthed and Modeled in Our Families

Before we ever experience our spiritual family, God's love is designed to be birthed and modeled in our natural families. This is ideally where we learn to be loved. Ephesians 5:18–6:4 describes being personally filled with the Spirit, and the apostle Paul also describes the natural family relationships that flow out of being filled with the Spirit. The family is a system in which children can grow up feeling loved, affirmed, and cared for—not for what they do but just for who they are.

As a result of being filled with the Spirit (Ephesians 5:18–20), we speak encouraging, uplifting, even melodious words to one another, giving thanks to God and submitting to each other as we submit to Jesus. No one demands their own way when the Spirit is in control. There's joy and freedom to let go in the knowledge that God is good and he loves us. We recognize him as the great choreographer of relationships and trust him to show us our part in the dance.

Paul then begins to describe family relationships. Husbands and wives are a picture of Jesus and his bride, the church, so wives should submit to their husbands, and husbands are to love their wives to the point of laying down their lives for them. Children are to obey their parents and honor them, and parents are to instruct their children in the things of the Lord and not frustrate them with impossible expectations. Families are to create an environment permeated with the love of God.

The point is that the Spirit, full of God's love, comes into the human heart, and the heart is meant to surrender to the Spirit's will and be influenced by his nature. That plays out in families as parents nurture their children. The mom shows her child that loving a husband means respecting him, encouraging him (and his sometimes fragile ego), affirming him, and trusting him. She may take some strong stands and challenge him sometimes, but she lets him know she's behind him one hundred percent.

The dad, feeling loved and empowered, shows his child what a husband's love is like—strong, sensitive, and sacrificial. He steps up to the family emotionally, spiritually, financially, and any other way the family needs to be led. He figures out what makes his wife feel loved, and then he does it. He becomes a living representation of Jesus.

Kids who can look up to their parents and see that kind of love grow up in a secure environment. They see their parents blow it and forgive each other, so they understand that love isn't performance oriented. They see affirmation for one another—not because of good behavior or the right image—but because of faithful commitment. They grow up with a good self-image because their family taught them that they are valuable simply for who they are. They have the freedom to be themselves, fully accepted and cherished without having to perform or manipulate to get the love they need. That's a picture of God's love, and it protects children from searching for substitutes when they are adults.

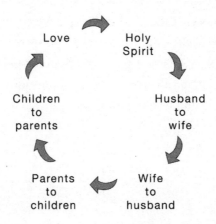

Genuine love in families is God's design, but it isn't the experience most of us have had. Most families, Christian or not, have not followed that design very well. My father and Theresa's father were both alcoholics. Good guys, just alcoholics. I never heard my father say "I love you" until he was in his late fifties and had been a Christian for a few years. I think I only saw my parents kiss twice when I was a kid. So I grew up looking for love in all the wrong places, just like most of you. The vast majority of us listen to the description of an ideal family and wish we could have grown up in that climate. But we aren't even sure how to provide that kind of climate for our children now.

The good news is that God is a God of grace. He gives second chances—and third, fourth, and a hundred and fourth chances too. He also knows how to fill in the gaps of our imperfections and make up for lost time. As soon as we move back toward his design, he meets us more than halfway. And whatever pains and dysfunctions we've experienced in the past can become an opportunity to experience his healing and love in new ways.

3. God Designed Love to Be Experienced When We Desperately Need It

The third way his love is worked into our lives has less to do with our relationships and more to do with timing. Somehow, we uniquely experience his love when we need it most desperately. Romans 5:3–5 tells us that we can rejoice in our sufferings because of what happens as a result. Trials and difficulties produce perseverance, which in turn develops character, which then gives us hope. And hope never disappoints because the Holy Spirit pours the love of God into our hearts.

We endure difficult, painful problems—a hard marriage, career frustration, a life-threatening illness—and something happens inside of us. We turn to God in ways we've never before sought him. Even when there's nothing to do, just hanging on develops something in us and draws us closer to him. As we trust God, our character changes, and as that happens, we begin to see the hope he has given us. We realize that he can change us, and he can also change circumstances. Our hope is received

> As we trust God, our character changes, and as that happens, we begin to see the hope he has given us.

when the Spirit of God—through the Word of God and in the context of community—pours out his love in our hearts. No matter what we've been through, whether it's an unthinkable loss, a betrayal, a tragedy, or a dysfunctional relationship, we can see that there's hope.

That's what Theresa had been through when I met her. She had a really painful childhood, looked for love in the wrong places and got married early, then was abandoned by her adulterous husband while she was pregnant with twins. But she persevered. She prayed and sang and cried out to God that she didn't have any money, or a future, or hope apart from him. By the time I met her a couple of years later, she had a precious, godly character like a piece of coal turned into a diamond. I saw her love and how she understood the amazing forgiveness of God, and it attracted me. I was drawn to her heart for him.

I had been on another route—the performance track. My love-receiver was searching for affirmation by getting A's, scoring points on the basketball court, and getting pretty girlfriends. To me, that would mean I was loved. Of course, it really left me empty. Nothing filled the hole. But that too was an opportunity to persevere, and out of my emptiness I found Christ. When we endure hard times and grow in character, we eventually experience God's love.

The spiritual family, the natural family, and our own

desperate times—these are the practical means of seeing, touching, and embracing God's love in our lives. At this point you might be nodding your head and saying in your heart, *That's what I want, but I don't know how.* Let me share a pathway—not a formula, but a practical path—to experience God's love in your life.

The Path to Experiencing God's Love

If you would really like to experience God's love, there is a very clear path to follow.

1. Step down. Surrender. Whether you're a Christian or not, you can choose to either live life on your agenda or on God's. A lot of people have made a decision to follow Christ but are still setting their own agenda. But if you want to fully connect with God, you'll need to make a definite decision: "Lord, from this day forward, I'm going to do it your way. I know it will be hard and I'll make mistakes, but whatever your Word says, however you lead, I'm doing life your way." Sometimes we only get there because the pain is so great there's nowhere else to go. That's fine—the way we get there isn't the issue. We just have to get there. Tell Christ from your heart, "I'm all in!"

2. Step away. We all walk in some kind of darkness. For me, it was hanging out in bars and drinking in the world's values. For you, it may be something entirely different. But when you move toward God, you almost always have to move away from certain people and other things that keep you in the darkness. If you're going to do life his way, you have to forsake doing it your way. And it really helps to start hanging out with other people who are committed to doing life his way.

3. Step in. No one can be a lone ranger Christian. In order to experience God's love, you have to live among a group of people who can speak truth and encouragement into your life. That's why we're so adamant about small groups at our church. Change happens in authentic community. It's impossible to meaningfully encounter God's love apart from deep, genuine connection and vulnerability with others. You have to let yourself be loved by people who have God's Spirit in them. That's risky, but the alternative is not being loved authentically—a much greater risk than being vulnerable with others who have chosen to be vulnerable too.

> No one can be a lone ranger Christian.

4. Step up. Once you've stepped into that community, there comes a time when you have to step up. You have to quit playing it safe and let people help you through your struggles. That means they will have to see the parts of you that aren't very pleasant. No one enjoys being that vulnerable, at least at first, but once you let go and realize people love you anyway, it's very liberating. I'm really proud of people when they say, "I'm an alcoholic and I need some people around me," or "I keep getting into dysfunctional relationships, and I'm the common denominator." They are ready to put the past behind and move up to the next level. They are stepping up and positioning themselves to experience God's love through others.

5. Step out. Eventually, you have to get your focus off yourself and onto others. Someone else is hurting more than you. Someone else is poorer or has a more difficult marriage problem or has a stronger addiction. When you start to give your life away by investing your time, energy, and resources in others, it will be given back to you. Do you really want to experience God's love? Then give it away. It will come back into your heart and life in greater measure.

Which of these steps do you need to take? Everyone in the world is trying to climb some kind of ladder looking for love—perfectionism, overachieving, fame, appearance . . . you name it. If there's some "one thing" that has to happen so you can be loved, maybe it's time to *step down* off that ladder and surrender—lock, stock, and barrel.

Or maybe you've done that and it's time to *step away*—out of the dark and into the light, getting away from the messages and messengers that keep you tied to the darkness. Stepping into the light may be a huge step away from an addiction. That may be alcohol or drugs, but it could really be anything—people's approval, fantasy football, or food. The options are limitless.

Perhaps your next step is the *step in*. You need to get with a group of people and figure what to share little by little as you open up your life to others. Or maybe this is the time for you to *step up*—to take that vulnerability to another level and expose some things you aren't very proud of, knowing that you'll benefit from the strengths of others around you who will accept you in spite of your flaws.

If you're on that journey, your next move is *stepping out*. It's time to get focused on helping other people.

Whichever step it is, it will require some faith. But anything in God's kingdom does. And it's always worth it. You're stepping into a deeper relationship with a God who is mighty to deliver, who delights in you, who will quiet you with his love, and who rejoices over you with singing. Even if you're afraid—a very common feeling among those who encounter God in scripture and are called to do great things—you can rest in the character of the one who has created you to experience his love.

How Do You Give God's Love Away?

Someone has wisely said that the only way to keep something is to give it away. Jesus taught the same in Luke 6:38. So let's learn how to give away the love we have received, because giving it is part of the experience. Paul gives us a glimpse in 1 Corinthians 13 of the kind of love that flows from God's heart and, when we're in tune with his Spirit, from ours. But like they say, a picture is worth a thousand words. Paul's description is words. The gospels give us a picture.

Jesus is the exact representation of God (Hebrews 1:3). That means that if God is love, Jesus is the exact representation of love. So if we want to know what it looks like to demonstrate God's love, all we need to do is look at Jesus. The best way to learn is by observation; our character is shaped far more power-

> If we want to know what it looks like to demonstrate God's love, all we need to do is look at Jesus.

fully by imitation than it is by instruction. We can't observe Jesus in person, of course—not in the natural, physical sense that his disciples were able to observe him. But we can get a pretty clear image of 1 Corinthians 13 by noticing how Jesus embodied love in the gospels. He shows us what love looks like. And not surprisingly, it's pretty simple!

So how did Jesus love the people around him—his family, friends, and enemies? I've listed eight ways:

1. He *talked* with them.

2. He *walked* with them.

3. He *ate* with them.

4. He *prayed* with them.

5. He *played* with them.

6. He *suffered* with them.

7. He *taught* them.

8. He *forgave* them.

Jesus talked with his family, friends, and enemies, walked with them, ate with them, prayed with them, laughed with them, cried with them, suffered with them, and rejoiced with them. He did that not only with his family and friends, but also with his enemies. He was never too busy to invest in the people who were right in front of him. He was fun to be around and fascinating to watch. He was real. People didn't know what he was going to do next. People liked being around him.

If we want to become loving people with our family, friends, and even our enemies, maybe that's a good model to follow. Maybe we should try talking, walking, eating, praying, laughing, crying, suffering, and rejoicing with them. Have fun, show love, and be the kind of person people want to be around. Drop some of the stuff that makes you so busy and do life with the people around you, just like Jesus did. If you do, those pressures that keep placing impossible demands on you will really start to shrink. When you love more, you will do less. And you won't need to go searching for love and find nothing but substitutes. Love—the real thing—will come to you.

QUESTIONS FOR
Reflection/Discussion

- In what ways is your life too busy because you are settling for "pseudo-love" substitutes?

- How deeply, on a scale of one to ten, do you feel loved by God? According to his Word and apart from your feelings, how deeply are you *actually* loved by him?

- What next step do you need to take to experience God's infinite love for you?

- Who in your family or circle of friends desperately needs to know God loves them? How specifically can you be a conduit of his love to them this week? To whom?

EIGHT

Love Train (Get on Board!)

*B*ack in the seventies, the O'Jays came out with a hit song called "Love Train." It encouraged people "all over the world" to join hands, start a love train, and let it ride. I'm not sure exactly what they had in mind, but it's a call to brothers and sisters all over the world to get on board. "You don't need a ticket" for this train, and "there ain't no war." Just join hands and make the world a better place.

The song struck a chord in those turbulent times of the cold war, nuclear arms, and racial tension. And even today when I hear this song, it brings a smile to my face as I tap my toe and sing along. You've probably heard it recently; it has become the theme song for a popular beer company, and they roll it out every year as soon as hot summer days call for their cold "silver bullet."

I chose this song to wrap up our journey together because I like the idea of a love train. Trains have tracks and destinations. People get on board with a destination in mind, and they arrive there together. And in this chapter, I want to look at the question of how to sustain spiritual simplicity over time. I want to explore God's "love train"—a supernatural community moving powerfully through history to bring life and love to people. He wants heaven to come down, for people to experience his kingdom and know that there's a real God who loves and cares about them. And he wants each of us on this train to invite more and more people onto it by how we live and what we do. This love train is the living, breathing body of Christ.

The tracks for this train are God's sovereign, unchanging, faithful purposes. He *will* fulfill his plan over time. He will glorify himself, bring all things under the rule and reign of Jesus, and cultivate a people to love him and be loved by him in a new heaven and earth forever.

The ticket for this train has already been purchased. Jesus paid for it on the cross for everyone who is willing to turn from their sin and believe. Accepting him by faith gives us a new life that goes on forever and ever, but the quality of this life starts now.

God is *the designer* of this train; he has been working on it from before the foundation of the world. The *engineer* is Jesus, the firstborn of the dead. He is the conductor who goes up and down the train checking on us and showing us all the stops. And where does the train stop? Wherever there's a human need. If someone is lonely, the train stops. If someone is discouraged or depressed, if someone has a financial or physical need, if someone is going through a relational crisis, that's where the train stops. And the Spirit who lives within us will speak the truth of God's Word through our lips and express God's love through our words and actions.

If you get on board this love train, you'll simplify your life. You'll stop *doing* so much and start *becoming* so much more. You won't need to seek approval from others or accumulate more stuff and status that won't mean anything at the end of your life. Your life will no longer be a temporal, trivial pursuit. It will be filled with meaning and purpose for eternity.

> If you get on board this love train, you'll simplify your life.

What Is Life Like on the Love Train?

For Christ's love compels us, because we are convinced that one died for all, and therefore all died. And he died for all, that those who live should no longer live for themselves but for him who died for them and was raised again. So from now on we regard no one from a worldly point of view. Though we once regarded Christ in this way, we do so no longer. Therefore, if anyone is in Christ, the new creation has come: The old has gone, the new is here! All this is from God, who reconciled us to himself through Christ and gave us the ministry of reconciliation: that God was reconciling the world to himself in Christ, not counting people's sins against them. And he has committed to us the message of reconciliation. We are therefore Christ's ambassadors, as though God were making his appeal through us. We implore you on Christ's behalf: Be reconciled to God. God made him who had no sin to be sin for us, so that in him we might become the righteousness of God. (2 Corinthians 5:14–21)

In his second letter to the Corinthians, Paul writes about all the trials and pain he has been through. It hasn't been an easy road; at times he's perplexed, discouraged, and under a lot of pressure. He has been beaten, ridiculed, imprisoned, and shipwrecked, but he keeps pressing ahead. He has been carrying around the death of Jesus within him, he says, so that other people can have the life of Jesus. In spite of everything, he still has hope and gratitude because he's focused on the unseen, not on what's visible. Amid all the adversity, he understands that life really matters only when you live with an eternal perspective.

So life on the love train isn't always easy, but there are some ways we can sustain it. And simplicity isn't about life being easier anyway; it's about life being less complex, more focused, and more meaningful. Doing less and loving more may be very difficult at first, but it isn't complicated at all. In these eight brief verses from 2 Corinthians 5, Paul reveals six core truths that allow us to sustain a lifestyle of spiritual simplicity. He shares what it takes to keep the train going.

> Paul reveals six core truths that allow us to sustain a lifestyle of spiritual simplicity.

1. Christ's love compels us (verse 14). Life on the love train isn't about trying hard. It isn't about religious activity or attempts at moral reform. It's about being connected with and surrendered to God's Spirit—getting into his Word and living in his community. Because we are convinced that Jesus died for all—and therefore, we all died with him—our new life is all for him, not for ourselves. Our love for him and his love for us and others gets inside of us, and that compels us to live selflessly for the good of others. We are motivated and directed by his love.

The word Paul uses for "compel" is actually a picture of being hemmed in. If you remember the first *Star Wars* movie, there's a scene where Luke, Princess Leia, and Han Solo are trapped in the Death Star's trash compactor and the walls start closing in. It looks like there's no way out. That "closing in" is the emotional picture Paul gives us of how Christ's love is hemming him in and compelling him—although in a much more positive, life-giving sense. It's good that there's no way out of this situation. Paul is so aware of God's love that he is absolutely compelled to apply it to the people around him. He sees the plight of people who don't know Christ's love, and the love within him compels him to respond to their needs.

2. Our life focus changes (verse 15). Christ's love changes our focus. Because we are convinced that Jesus died for us,

LOVE TRAIN (GET ON BOARD!)   169

we no longer live for ourselves. That's what surrender is about. We don't just make Jesus part of our life. He becomes the central focus, the reason we get up in the morning, the motivation behind how we spend our time, our money, and our energy, and the basis for all our relationships. We don't live for ourselves anymore. We live for him.

So we no longer ask questions like "What will make me happy?" or "What can I do with my time?" We ask questions like "How can I further his agenda?" or "What do I do with the time he has entrusted to me?" How we raise our kids, how we spend our money, how we invest ourselves in other people—all of it is now centered around him. That's a radical change for most of us, but that's what it means to simplify your life on the Love Train. Our entire focus changes. We experience a new power and peace.

3. We get new eyes (verse 16). When we are living for Jesus and not for ourselves, we get new eyes. We no longer look at people from a worldly point of view. The color of their skin, their background, their cool factor, their personal hygiene, their personality quirks—none of that is their identity. That's what God told the prophet Samuel when he went to anoint a new king to eventually replace King Saul. The sons of Jesse who looked like they had king potential—the big, strong, good-looking guys with obvious leadership qualities—were brought before Samuel, but God said no to all of them. He told Samuel, "Do not consider his appearance or his height, for I have rejected him. The Lord does not look at the things man looks at. Man looks at the outward appearance, but the Lord looks at the heart" (1 Samuel 16:7). Finally God brought Samuel to the youngest in the family—the shepherd David.

When we're on the love train, we stop looking at outward appearances and stop measuring by worldly standards. We start looking at where people are really coming from. We see them not according to their past or even their present, but according to their potential in Christ. We look past their struggles and baggage and backgrounds and notice the inside beauty. We have new eyes for others and measure their value differently.

> We see others not according to their past or even their present, but according to their potential in Christ.

4. We get new hope (verse 17). If anyone is in Christ, he is a new creation. The old has passed away and the new has come. We quote this verse often about our new life in Christ when we turn from our sin and receive him as Savior. We actually become a new creation. But in the context of this passage, it's really saying we don't look at people externally anymore. Our new eyes tell us that no person or situation is beyond the love and redemption of Christ.

When you're on the love train and the love of God is pulsating through your veins, you don't see the same old people. You see the potential of new creatures. All the things we thought God could never forgive—the addictions we thought were too tough to break, the people who prompted us to say, "Well, leopards don't change their spots"—it's all history. God can do anything. He *wants* to do amazing things. He is the God of impossibilities; nothing is too difficult for him. Change is what the gospel is all about. And we get in on it!

5. We get a new responsibility (verses 18–19). The love train is not a sit-back-and-enjoy-the-ride cruise through the countryside, and it's not just a nonstop ticket to heaven. It's a hang-on-to-your-seats adventure that involves a lot of combat and endurance. Remember the context Paul has in mind as he writes? He's been through a lot. There's a spiritual war going on, and God has equipped his people to get out into the battlefield and rescue people.

So we have a new responsibility that Paul calls "the ministry of reconciliation." The word "reconciled" simply means to become friends with someone. We've been reconciled to

God through Jesus, and then he gives us the same ministry to others. He has been reconciling the world to himself and not counting people's sins against them. Our message isn't "Clean your life up and start coming to church and reading the Bible." It's this: "God has placed your sins on Christ. Your ticket on the love train has already been purchased. God loves you and wants you on board."

Most people who are honest will tell you that their efforts to run their own lives aren't going very well. Most marriages aren't as fulfilling as they were meant to be, most parenting isn't going as expected, most people's financial situation isn't very secure, and most people aren't thrilled with where their career is headed. And if you do find someone for whom life is going really well, you may be surprised to hear how many feel really empty in spite of their successes.

God has called us to meet people where they are and be winsome, loving, and focused on their needs. Our ministry of reconciliation is to tell people that God loves them, that he is inviting them into relationship with him. On the basis of Christ's work on the cross, he doesn't count their sins against them and they can receive forgiveness! That's what it means to bring good news.

   6. *We get a new role (verses 20–21)*. We are Christ's ambassadors, sent out into the world as though God were mak-

ing his appeal through us. This is God's message: "I want to be friends with people. Sin is a barrier. I've removed the barrier, so now we can be friends." It's like a married couple who have separated or divorced and then decide to be reconciled. God wants to reconcile everyone to himself and, like ambassadors who represent their home country while they live in another country, we go out and represent his interests. Our citizenship is in heaven, which is where we're headed if we're on the love train.

God wants us to seep like liquid into every kind of need, to love people wherever they are without judging them, to simply tell them the truth. But he doesn't

> God wants us to seep like liquid into every kind of need.

call us just to speak words; he calls us to put our arm around them, help them, and show them this is how a loving God responds to them.

Paul is really giving us a powerfully vivid picture here. Verse 21 tells us that God made Christ, who was sinless, to become sin for us so that we might become the righteousness of God in him. In other words, he exchanged lives with us. He took our old one to the grave and gave us his life as our new one. So as ambassadors, we have a standing before God that is identical to Jesus' standing before him. He sees us as completely righteous—as his own sons and daughters.

That's amazing! Awesome! Mind-boggling! Don't skip over this if it's new territory, and don't blow past this truth if it's the old familiar ground of justification. Let it sink in. Drink it up. We are sons and daughters, deeply, eternally loved, and commissioned and empowered to share this good news with everyone everywhere.

This is why the love of Christ compelled Paul. He was a very religious man until he met Jesus and realized how broken he was. Then he met Jesus personally on the Damascus road and became a passionate follower of this living Christ who has unlimited power. And that same power that was able to raise Jesus from the dead worked in him—and works in us if we are his followers.

So that's how we sustain spiritual simplicity—six core truths that summarize our life and journey on the love train. We are connected with a living Savior. We don't live under a bunch of "shoulds" and "oughts" because we're compelled by his love. We don't live for ourselves anymore. We have a new focus and live for him. We don't see the same way anymore because we have new eyes. And we don't lose heart in any situation because we have hope for everyone we meet. No one is beyond his power or love, no matter where they have been or what they have done. We have a new responsibility that goes way beyond making sure the kids have good SAT scores or moving upward in our career path. There may be many important responsibilities in our lives, but our core responsibility is to be an ambassador, a representative of the all-powerful, all-knowing, infinitely loving, living God. First in our homes, and then all around us.

There are plenty of ways to do that. God has given us all kinds of gifts and dreams and desires, and each of us has several roles to fulfill: mom, dad, husband, wife, brother, sister, nephew, niece, accountant, developer, designer, bricklayer . . . and on and on. But above all of these desires and roles is our seat on the love train and our calling to reconcile people to God.

How Does Life on the Love Train Really Work?

That's the picture and the theology behind it. But what's the game plan? How does this really work?

Picture Jesus walking into the room right now and standing in front of you. Imagine having an emotional venting session with him. You just blurt out all the stresses, pressures, anxieties, fears, hopes, dreams, ambitions that have been churning around inside of you. You give him all the details of how crazy life is—of all the turmoil that's in the world as a whole and in your personal life. Then you ask him this one question: "Lord, what do you want me to do?"

What do you think he would say?

I think he would say, "Love God, and love people." That's it. That's how simple life is meant to be. Sure, you've got to eat and pay the bills, but he'll help with the details. And

> "Love God, and love people." That's it. That's how simple life is meant to be.

those really are details. The more important things are relationships, and the most important aspect of relationships is love. Not love expressed by buying more or doing more, but love expressed in quality time, emotional engagement, and lives invested in one another. It isn't very complicated.

In fact, that's pretty much what Jesus said when someone asked him which commandment was the greatest. He said there are actually two: "Love the Lord your God with all your heart and with all your soul and with all your mind and with all your strength. The second is this: Love your neighbor as yourself. There is no commandment greater than these" (Mark 12:30–31). The ultimate test of success and spiritual maturity is loving God more deeply and authentically each day. And as a result of that love, we love others more sincerely and more practically each day in ways that are meaningful to them.

This is not a onetime decision. It's a lifestyle. It involves reorienting your perspective and, when necessary, rearranging life itself. You may need to get rid of some things in your life, and you may need to add some others. Whatever it takes to line yourself up with God and his agenda of love, it's worth doing.

The Profile of a Disciple

We talk a lot at our church about being a Romans 12 Christian. I think that chapter is one of the best glimpses in scripture of what it looks like to love God and others as a lifestyle. It tells us how to relate appropriately to God, to the world, to ourselves, to other Christians, and to those outside the church, even our enemies.

It all begins in *verse 1* with surrender to God. We offer ourselves to him as a living sacrifice. That's what true worship looks like—reorienting ourselves around him so that he becomes the focus of our lives.

Then in *verse 2*, we refuse to be conformed to the world and its ways. That's the "step away" we talked about in the last chapter. As we do that, our minds are renewed, and then we're able to understand and demonstrate what God's will is.

In *verses 3–8*, we undertake a sober self-assessment.

This is how to view ourselves accurately. We don't get too inflated, but we know how valuable we are as people of faith and members of the body of Christ. We have different gifts, all vital to how the body functions.

Verses 9–13 describe the character of love—how we serve. Our love is to be sincere, without hypocrisy. We hate evil and cling to good. We don't just come to events at church; we do life together. We're devoted to each other. We give preference to each other in honor. We lay our lives out for one another. We love each other in such a way that people outside can't understand. It's not an organization; it's a living organism of people connected to God and to people who serve each other.

And then *verses 14–21* describe our responses of love to those who oppose us. We supernaturally respond to evil with good. When our enemies need food, we feed them. When they're thirsty, we give them something to drink. When they harm us, we don't take revenge. Instead, we overcome evil with goodness.

That's it. Love God, love others. That's what it looks like for a Christian who has learned to live simply.

The <u>Profile</u> of a <u>Disciple</u>

⊞ Surrendered to God

⊞ Separate from world's values

⊞ Sober self-assessment

⊞ Serving in love

⊞ Supernaturally responding to evil with good

The Practices of a Disciple

Saying this lifestyle is simple isn't the same as saying it's easy. It isn't easy at all. But if we adopt three practices and follow them in dependency and faith, God gives us the grace to become who we need to become.

> Saying this lifestyle is simple isn't the same as saying it's easy.

In our church and at Living on the Edge, we have simplified all the spiritual disciplines and activities down to three prepositions. We call it BIO: **B**efore God, **I**n community, **O**n mission 24/7.

Before God. We will never be the kind of Christian who fits the profile if we aren't coming before God daily and spending time in his Word. Talking with Him and listening to his voice, we must all learn to surrender daily. There is a certain time when you make a decision to be "all in," like we discussed in the last chapter. But it isn't *just* a onetime decision. It's a lifestyle, an ongoing commitment. This is the worship of Romans 12:1, our willingness to be a living sacrifice.

That means that whatever he says in his Word, we've already committed to doing it—not only when it looks like it's going to work out well for us, but also when we really don't want to do it. By faith we believe what he says about handling money, what he says about how to do relationships and what boundaries to put around them, what he says about sacrifice, and what he says about everything else. Sometimes we see the benefits of his ways—his Word will keep us out of debt, protect us from sexually transmitted diseases, and help us stay married for the long haul—and sometimes we don't. We choose by faith to obey, even when obedience looks hard.

The truth is that radical obedience isn't just hard; it's impossible. We can't do it on our own. But as we immerse ourselves in God's Word, talk with him in prayer, and stay in relationship with his people, he gives us the grace to do it. Grace creates in us the desire and the power to do his will. And it becomes more real in our experience as we consciously live our lives with the awareness that we are before God every moment of every day.

This is more than just having a devotional life. It includes coming before him regularly on a weekend to worship with others, but it's much more than that. It's being before God daily—talking with him wherever you are, uttering quick prayers before meetings, asking him to help with whatever problems you're having or temptations you need to overcome, experiencing his presence . . . in other words, bringing him into every area of life as a living reality. It's a practice that requires some discipline at first, but over time it becomes very natural.

In community. Living out spiritual simplicity is impossible alone. Everyone needs to have deep relationships with other believers. This involves being in a small group, but it's more than that. It's doing life with a group of people who really know you and love you, and you know them and love them. Authenticity thrives when everyone takes off their masks—it's when the real you meets real needs for the right reason in the right way. When someone in the group has a need and you spend money or give time sacrificially, God's grace overflows into his or her life and into yours. Loneliness is the number one malady in American culture.

Religious programs, classes, and spiritual disciplines all have their place. But transformation requires heart-to-heart, face-to-face, sacrificial life in community.

> Transformation requires heart-to-heart, face-to-face, sacrificial life in community.

On mission. Disciples on the love train are always on mission. It doesn't matter whether you're at your job, at the gym, at the store, or at home. Wherever there's a crisis or a need, you have the potential to be one of God's answers to it. Living "on mission" means asking the Spirit to give you wisdom wherever you go each and every day so you'll know how to serve and reach out as a minister of reconciliation. You are a full-time ambassador from heaven, on call 24/7.

These practices aren't new, and they aren't complicated, but they are neglected by surprisingly many believers. And they make sense, don't they? The Christian life is simple, not complicated. It's not simplistic, but it's clear, relational, and dynamic. Unfortunately, it isn't working for a lot of people because they've put it into their minds and hearts without actually putting it into practice. One reason for that is that many people don't understand the spiritual turning points that lead to genuine change.

Three Spiritual Turning Points—
and the Fears That Keep Us from Them

Let's look a little deeper into the three spiritual turning points we just discussed: *Before God (Surrender), In Community, On Mission.*

1. Surrender

We've talked a lot about this word in the last few pages, but it's worth emphasizing because I get hundreds of e-mails from people who have been Christians for years saying, "I've never heard about surrender, but I prayed today to be 'all in,' and I can't believe how my life has changed." Marriages are restored, finances get under control, and people start to find the meaning and purpose they've been looking for. Radical, amazing things begin to happen.

So why doesn't everyone radically surrender to God? Because we have certain phobias associated with giving up control of our lives. We're afraid that God's plan for our lives will fall short of the life we've envisioned for ourselves. We falsely assume that if we have money, we'll have to give it all up. If we're single, we'll always be single. If we're in a career we really like, we'll have to serve in a way that isn't as fulfilling. We're under some illusion that we know what outcomes are best for our lives and that we know the best way to get those outcomes. In a word, we refuse to surrender to God because we fear what the future might hold for us under his direction.

Think about how illogical that is. We're talking about the all-knowing, all-powerful God who loves us so much and is so on our side that he gave his Son to die on the cross for us. Does he really not know what's best for us? Would he really go to such great lengths on our behalf and then hold out on us? No, if he gave us the life of his Son, he will certainly do what's best for us in every area of life (Romans 8:32). He is not the "hard master" many people fear.

But most research about religious practices in America reveals that nine out of ten Christians are not "all in." And when we're not surrendered completely, when we're living for ourselves and not for him, we limit the flow of God's Spirit. We aren't compelled by the love of Christ or experiencing his presence. There's no power in our lives. The Christian life becomes a set of principles to live by at best, and impossible rules to keep at worst.

"The Lord God is a sun and shield; the Lord bestows favor and honor; no good thing does he withhold" (Psalm 84:11).

Look at what God promises us. "The Lord God is a sun and shield; the Lord bestows favor and honor; no good thing does he withhold from those whose walk is blameless" (Psalm 84:11). Surrender is the true channel through which God's biggest and best blessings flow. In other words, we'll get the best by surrendering. A little Bible reading, a little churchgoing, a little involvement in Christian activity—that level of investment is not going to result in any power in our lives. But going all in with God ignites radical change that lasts.

To summarize:

- spiritual turning point = surrender

- action = "I'm all in!"

- inhibitor = fear of the future

- key passage = Psalm 84:11

- result = spiritual power

2. In Community

We emphasize the importance of authentic community because life change only happens in the context of deep, honest, vulnerable relationships. This is why Jesus modeled doing life in a small group. It was in this environment that the disciples and early church were transformed. But we have a phobia in this area too—the fear of rejection. This fear can undermine our relationships with others because it keeps us from sharing who we really are.

I've seen this again and again. I've been in small groups where nothing substantial happens. We may talk about the Bible a little, but everyone stays superficial. We have some coffee, socialize, and maybe touch on some areas of need. But the fear of rejection keeps members working hard to present their best selves. That falls short of God's goal for Christian community.

Every small group that becomes an authentic experience of community does so when someone has some courage. At some point, someone says, "You know, I've never shared this ugly part of my life before, but I need to work through some things, and I feel safe enough with you to do that." They become vulnerable and put their issues out there for others to see.

There's a real fear of rejection in doing that. If someone gets shut down, that person may stuff the issues back inside and never take them out again. Putting them out there is a step of faith. It's a different kind of surrender—the surrender of an image. You let people see who you really are.

Rejection doesn't usually happen in this situation. Usually, people say, "Wow, you struggle with that too?" And suddenly the dynamics of the group change. Defenses come down and people get real, and God's Spirit begins to bring healing and restoration as truth replaces image management.

> God's Spirit begins to bring healing and restoration as truth replaces image management.

The alternative is to keep putting forth a false image that isn't really you. Even if that attracts love, it's love based on an illusion. If you never risk rejection, you'll never really be loved. But when you wisely share the real you and your real struggles with people who have demonstrated they can be trusted, and those people look you in the eye and love you anyway, healing takes place. That's a vital key to life change, and it's why we're commanded to "accept one another, just as Christ accepted you, in order to bring praise to God" (Romans 15:7).

To summarize:

- spiritual turning point = vulnerability

- action = "I'm taking off my mask"

- inhibitor = fear of rejection

- key passage = Romans 15:7

- result = acceptance, love, and healing

3. On Mission

When we step out and serve, we become the conduit of the grace of God. But there's a phobia associated with stepping out: the fear of failure. Maybe we'll fall flat on our face. Maybe we'll look foolish. Maybe we'll end up doing more harm than good. But is that very realistic? Can we really fail when God is with us?

The first time I led someone to Christ, I did it very poorly. I stumbled over my words, and I was going so slowly that the guy finally interrupted and asked if he could go ahead and receive Christ. I didn't even know how to pray with him, so I stumbled through that too. But it was real, and that young man's life was changed for all eternity. God took over.

Being on mission with God doesn't just mean leading people to Christ. Maybe it's helping restore a marriage, changing a tire, befriending a neighbor, or even just telling someone who is going through a hard time that God sees and cares. It's consciously seeking to love, to be a conduit of God's grace to bring life, hope, and healing to others. Whatever the context, when you sense God working through you and you re-

> When you sense God working through you and you realize it's him, not you, it's wonderfully addicting.

alize it's him, not you, it's wonderfully addicting. It feels electric. You'll begin to take risks like never before. As you grow, you'll learn and discover the specific gifts God has given you to be his hands and feet and lips to those around you. "Each one should use whatever gift he has received to serve others, faithfully administering God's grace in its various forms" (1 Peter 4:10).

Every time I watch people take these steps of faith, amazing things happen. They ignite life change. These processes aren't easy—the life of faith never is—but God honors our commitment to him. If we're persistent in our faith, we eventually see the fruit of it.

To summarize:

- spiritual turning point = serving

- action = "I'm using my gifts"

- inhibitor = fear of failure

- key passage = 1 Peter 4:10

- result = impact

An Invitation to All

If I could figure out how to sit across from every person reading this book and listen to you talk about your spiritual journey, I would encourage you to simplify your life, to make room to come *before God* daily, to do life *in community* weekly, and to be *on mission* 24/7. I would take a sip of my coffee to gather some courage, and then I'd look you in the eye with deep compassion and hope and challenge you to face those fears. I'd remind you that we all have them, and many of our fast-paced, shallow relationships are the way we're wrongly dealing with these fears. I would remind you one more time that love is what really matters, urging you to stop doing so much and take time to love more. Finally, I would stay up late into the night telling you one story after another of people's lives changing as they take these steps of faith.

So my invitation is to get on board the love train and spend your life receiving God's love and demonstrating it to others. Jesus issued a similar invitation, and it comes with some profound promises of a simpler life:

> Come to me, all you who are weary and burdened, and I will give you rest. Take my yoke upon you and learn from me, for I am gentle and humble in heart,

*and you will find rest for your souls. For my yoke is
easy and my burden is light.* (Matthew 11:28–30)

In other words, "Do life my way. I've got your best in mind, and I'll give rest for your souls."

If you've been building your life on a foundation of something other than love, you may wonder if it's too late to take steps radical enough to do less and love more. After all, it's impossible to replace a foundation once a building has been built. But what is impossible physically is possible spiritually. God really does give us that opportunity in our lives. Some structures and supports may need to change, but you don't have to go back and start building life from the ground up. Start from where you are and base your life on love and see what happens. You'll find that as your motivation changes, your life takes on a more elegant, less cluttered look. It becomes richer and more meaningful.

It also becomes more beautiful. When you know how deeply you are loved by God, you will naturally overflow with love for others. People are drawn to those who are loving. Relationships deepen. The meaning of life becomes clearer.

Life may be hard sometimes, but it really isn't as complicated as we make it out to be. The race for bigger-better-faster-more is never-ending and exhausting. It drains us of energy and robs us of joy. But the life of love yields visible fruit and gives us energy and joy. We will never regret investing ourselves in what really matters—the relationships God has placed in our lives. And when we choose to do less and love more, we'll find that we actually end up accomplishing more—not more activity but more of what lasts for eternity. The fulfillment we seek in so many ways can only be found when we slow down, refocus, and decide to simply love.

Acknowledgments

A very special thank-you to our good God who allowed my wife Theresa to go through cancer as I was working on this manuscript. He showed us both in fresh and powerful ways how important loving relationships are and how secondary is all else. We are grateful cancer is in the rearview mirror, but can't discount the precious time with Christ and one another on the journey.

We also want to thank the leadership and congregation of Venture Christian Church where these messages were birthed and the team at Living on the Edge that created and distributed this content on radio and small-group DVD curriculum.

A special thanks to Philis for her encouragement and

editing and to Jonathan and the Howard team for their patience and flexibility after cancer interfered with deadlines.

Thank you Curtis and all the Yates and Yates Team, for your decade of perseverance and belief in me and God's message through me.

Finally I want to thank a conference speaker I drove to the airport when I was a student. He challenged my view of the church and later my understanding of 1 Corinthians 13. I met him only once, but his three cassette teachings of twenty years ago launched my journey of what love looks like in real life. Thanks Tim.

Notes

1. Jim Dethmer, teaching series, "The Supremacy of Love."

2. Ibid.

3. To discover how to develop a sober self-assessment, go to www.LivingontheEdge.org/r12online.

4. Dethmer.